BEFORE THE KNOT

ESSENTIAL INSIGHTS FOR A SUCCESSFUL MARRIAGE

BY

LA. SMITH

TABLE OF CONTENTS

CHAPTER ONE .... - 1 -

UNDERSTANDING YOURSELF .... - 1 -

CHAPTER TWO .... - 24 -

MINDFUL OR LUSTFUL UNION .... - 24 -

CHAPTER THREE .... - 35 -

COMPATIBILITY AND SHARED VALUES .... - 35 -

CHAPTER FOUR .... - 48 -

THE PSYCHOLOGICAL ASPECT OF RELATIONSHIPS .... - 48 -

CHAPTER FIVE .... - 75 -

RELATIONSHIP RED FLAGS AND BEHAVIOR PATTERN .... - 75 -

CHAPTER SIX .... - 91 -

SUPERFICIAL, DEEP AND SPIRITUAL CONNECTIONS .... - 91 -

CHAPTER SEVEN .... - 111 -

DIFFERENTIATING INFATUATION FROM DELUSION .... - 111 -

CHAPTER EIGHT .... - 125 -

COMMUNICATION AND CONFLICT RESOLUTION .... - 125 -

CHAPTER NINE .... - 152 -

FINANCES AND SHARED RESPONSIBILITIES .... - 152 -

CHAPTER TEN .... **- 174 -**

RESILIENCE AND ADAPTABILITY .... - 174 -

CHAPTER ELEVEN .... **- 194 -**

FAMILY AND SUPPORT SYSTEM IN MARRIAGE .... - 194 -

CHAPTER TWELVE .... **- 213 -**

REASONS WHY 50% OF MARRIAGES OR RELATIONSHIPS FAIL .... - 213 -

CONCLUSION .... **- 231 -**

DEDICATION

I would like to dedication this book to my son and daughter. To my beloved Son Quinton and Daughter Cheridan Jones: As you both embark on your journeys in this world, I dedicate this book to you with all my heart. Within these pages, I have explored the intricacies of self-discovery and understanding yourself and future partner before marriage, essential elements for building a successful and enduring relationship.

Sharing your Love and choosing a life partner is indeed a choice and one of the most important decisions of your life. It is my sincerest hope that the insights shared in this book will serve as a guiding light for you both as you navigate the complexities of love and partnership in your own lives.

With all my love and best wishes,

L.A Smith

PRELUDE

MY STORY: THE ILLUSION OF PERFECTION

I was married to a man I believed was my soul-mate for two decades, and I thought I had love all figured out. My life before marriage was filled with a series of golden achievements. I always excelled in my academic pursuits, graduating the top of my classes in High School, Magna Cum Laude in my undergraduate studies, and sustaining a perfect 4.0 GPA during my master's program. Excellence was not just an outcome; it was my identity. My oldest sister often showered me with praise; she would say with a big smile, "Everything you touch turns to gold," a phrase that became both a compliment and a prophecy I endeavored to fulfill. Everything seemed perfect, and I expected my marriage to be just as successful. But unfortunately, that wasn't the case!

Who would have thought this was going to happen to me? I didn't quite give marriage much thought; I always believed it was something I could also achieve perfectly. But as I look back, I see even more clearly how natural it was to expect my marriage to gleam with the same luster as everything else in my life. I had always been successful in everything I did, and I couldn't understand why my marriage couldn't be the same. The realization that my marriage was failing hit me (hard). It was a painful awareness that I tried to ignore for a long time. I made excuses for my own behavior and tolerance. I also made excuses for my husband's behavior, thinking that it was just a phase and that he would eventually come around. But I was wrong. The man I fell in love with, the one I thought was my (forever partner, had changed. He was no longer the caring, loving husband I had married. Instead, he was distant, uncommunicative, and emotionally unavailable.

In my marriage, I experienced both wonderful moments and challenging times. I later realized that the complexities of marriage were far beyond my initial understanding. While I had been successful in various aspects of my life, navigating the intricacies of a relationship revealed a whole new set of skills and insights that I had yet to develop. It became clear to me that true success in marriage required more than just external achievements; it demanded emotional intelligence, communication skills, empathy, and a willingness to grow and adapt together. As I reflected on my journey, I understood that marriage was a continuous learning process that required constant effort, understanding, and a deep connection with my partner. The big question is, are you willing and capable to do the work?

It is clear to me now that marriage went beyond the everyday tasks of working, providing, cooking, cleaning, and caring for the kids. It was more than just enjoying vacations, having fun, and intimacy. Marriage also encompassed personal growth, self-discovery, discipline, and nurturing each other. It was about evolving together, supporting each other's development, and truly becoming a unified force in our daily lives. This realization opened my eyes to the deeper layers of connection and commitment that marriage entails, highlighting the importance of continuous growth, mutual understanding, and shared goals in building a strong and fulfilling partnership.

In hindsight, had I possessed the wisdom I have today, I would have understood that selecting a life partner transcends mere affection. For me, it would involve recognizing and applying all the invaluable insights presented in this book to discern the ideal companion. Someone who not only meets the evolving challenges but also embraces growth hand in hand every step of the journey. Both of us must grasp the significance of this groundwork and be dedicated to the mutual effort required.

It signifies a pledge, a dedication... a covenant, collaboration, with love as the ultimate reward.

INTRODUCTION

EXPLORING LOVE, COMPATIBILITY, AND COMMITMENT

Marriage is a sacred union between two individuals who commit to spending their lives together. It's a bond built on love, self-discovery, and commitment. Before deciding to tie the knot, exploring what these three things mean to you is crucial. Love is a journey that can be described as a winding path filled with unexpected twists, exhilarating highs, and heart-wrenching lows. For some, love starts with a chance encounter, a shared glance that sparks a connection. For others, it evolves slowly, progressing from friendship into something more profound. I remember the time when I was deeply in love with someone. It was a beautiful feeling, and it made me feel alive. Every moment spent together felt like a treasure, and I couldn't imagine my life without that person. We exchanged vows, and we were happily in love. However, despite its beauty and promise, love is also a journey fraught with challenges, uncertainties, and difficult choices. As time passed, I realized that love alone was not enough. We were incompatible, and our shared commitment was not strong enough to sustain the relationship. Eventually, we went our separate ways, which was a painful experience. But why? You may be wondering why, if we loved each other, we couldn't make it work?

As much as love is the foundation of every successful marriage, it alone is not enough to sustain one. Marriage requires teamwork to overcome challenges. Unfortunately, my partner and I struggled to keep up with each other's rhythm, and my unrealistic expectations were shattered against the harsh rocks of reality. This difficult experience taught me a valuable lesson that every couple should understand. Love alone is not enough to sustain a healthy relationship. Marriage comes with many responsibilities, and love is undoubtedly a priority. Yet, it's essential to understand that this feeling can fade away. What will be left after that? This is where compatibility and shared commitment come into play. These pillars hold a relationship together, even when the initial rush of emotions fades away.

Compatibility and shared commitment are two fundamental aspects of a successful and fulfilling marriage. Compatibility involves the ability of two individuals to coexist and thrive together. At the same time, shared commitment is the dedication and loyalty that binds them together in their journey through life. Before you say your vows, it's essential to understand what compatibility and shared commitment mean in marriage. Compatibility goes beyond physical attraction and shared interests; it involves emotional, social, and intellectual alignment. You must be able to communicate effectively with your partner, share common values and goals, and feel comfortable being around them. On the other hand, shared commitment is the willingness to work together towards a common goal - building a life together. It involves being there for each other through thick and thin, supporting each other's dreams and aspirations, and being willing to make sacrifices for the sake of the relationship.

Love is not just about emotions and feelings; it's also about actions and commitments. As described by 1 Corinthians 13:6-8, love does not take pleasure in wrongdoing or evil actions but instead finds joy in truth and righteousness. Love is a protective force that always trusts, hopes, and perseveres. It's a constant and enduring force that never fails. This means that love is both a fleeting emotion and a steadfast commitment to care for and support others. It also emphasizes the enduring nature of love; love never fails, implying that it is a constant force that remains strong and unwavering. That's the kind of love we should strive for in our relationships - a love built on repetitive and intentional behaviors that foster personal growth and healthy relationships. That's where this book comes in. It's a powerful resource that explores key aspects everyone should understand before saying "I do."

It's an engaging and emotional read that will equip you with essential insights to effectively walk down the aisle prepared for the vows you want to exchange. The book covers everything you need, from assessing your compatibility and shared commitment with your partner to having open and honest conversations about your values, goals, and expectations. These discussions will help you ensure that you both have the same understanding of important issues such as finances, children, and career aspirations.

So, what are you waiting for? Let's dive in!

IT'S TIME TO LEARN!

GRAB A CUP OF TEA AND LEARN!

CHAPTER ONE

UNDERSTANDING YOURSELF

HAVE YOU EVER FOUND yourself asking the question, "Who am I?" This question had been persistently nagging at me, and I couldn't shake it off. I felt like I was losing touch with my identity and slipping away into the shadows of other people's expectations. I had been ignoring the subtle signs trying to tell me that I was not living the life I wanted. I kept pushing down my inner voice, hoping that if I just tried harder, everything would fall into place. But as time went by, I felt more and more distant from the person I once knew. I buried my emotions and desires beneath layers of obligation and duty, pretending that everything was fine with a plastered-on smile. Deep down, I knew I was suffocating under the weight of unspoken truths and unfulfilled dreams.

When I looked in the mirror, I didn't recognize the person staring back at me. I had lost touch with the vibrant and confident woman I once was. I felt powerless to change the course of my life and voiceless about my own needs and desires. It was then that I finally realized that I needed to understand myself, reclaim my identity, and chart my own path forward. I couldn't continue living a life that wasn't mine, shackled by expectations and obligations. How did I do this? It was through a deep self-reflection and becoming self-aware. Through this process, I learned a lot about myself and how to move forward in my life with purpose. Let's delve into this in detail including how it could pertain to your marriage.

Self-reflection and Self-awareness

Self-reflection and self-awareness are indispensable components in the journey of personal growth and development. They demand that we take a moment to introspectively examine our thoughts, feelings, and behaviors and understand our strengths, weaknesses, values, and beliefs.

Self-reflection is a process that allows us to look inward and analyze our experiences, actions, and motivations. It enables us to gain insight into ourselves, our relationships, and our world. When we reflect on ourselves, we can identify patterns in our behavior, recognize areas for improvement, and make more informed decisions about our lives. On the other hand, self-awareness is recognizing and understanding our emotions, thoughts, and behaviors and how they impact ourselves and others. It involves being mindful of our strengths and weaknesses, values and beliefs, and goals and aspirations. Self-awareness allows us to navigate our emotions better, communicate effectively with others, and make choices that align with our values and goals.

Together, self-reflection and self-awareness empower us to live more intentionally and authentically. They enable us to cultivate a deeper understanding of ourselves, improve our relationships with others, and pursue personal and professional growth with clarity and purpose. So, take some time out and reflect on yourself to become the best version of you.

Self-reflection and Self-awareness in Marriage

In any marriage or relationship, it is crucial to cultivate self-reflection and self-awareness. When you take the time to reflect on your needs, wants, and limitations, you will gain a deeper understanding of yourself and your partners. This, in turn, will help you establish a strong foundation for a healthy and long-lasting marriage. Here is a detailed exploration of how self-reflection and self-awareness play a vital role in a successful marriage:

The Role of Self-Reflection in Marriage

Self-reflection is a crucial aspect of any marriage. It involves taking a step back and analyzing your actions, reactions, and underlying motivations in your relationship. It's about understanding why you respond to certain situations in specific ways and considering how your background, experiences, and personal issues contribute to your behavior in the relationship.

In a marriage, self-reflection can help partners identify patterns in their behavior that may contribute to feelings of frustration or resentment. For instance, let's take the example of Nicole and Mark, a couple who have been married for a few years and have been experiencing recurring arguments about the division of household chores. Nicole often finds herself overwhelmed with managing the house and caring for their children, while Mark feels he's doing his fair share, but Nicole doesn't appreciate it. Through self-reflection, Nicole can explore why she gets so frustrated when Mark doesn't help with chores as much as she would like. She may realize that her childhood experiences of seeing her mother bear the brunt of household duties have influenced her expectations in her marriage.

Understanding this will help her better comprehend how her past informs her present behavior, and she can try to adjust accordingly. In addition, Nicole can reflect on how her need for control and perfectionism impacts her reactions to the situation. She might acknowledge that she struggles to delegate tasks and express her needs clearly, which leads to resentment building up over time. This means that Nicole becomes more self-aware and can work on changing her behavior to see things more clearly, be receptive to Mark's concerns, and appreciate his efforts. Here are other vital roles self-reflection plays in Marriage:

Understanding Emotional Reactions

One crucial aspect of self-reflection in marriage is understanding our emotional reactions to various situations. In a marriage, emotions can run high, and it's easy to get caught up in the heat of the moment. And often, our immediate responses are influenced by past experiences, unmet needs, and underlying beliefs. However, by taking a few moments to reflect on our emotional response to a situation, we can gain insight into what's happening beneath the surface and why we react the way we do. This can help us communicate our needs and feelings more effectively, leading to a deeper understanding and connection with our partners. For example, if a spouse feels triggered by a seemingly innocuous comment, self-reflection can help uncover the underlying insecurities or past wounds contributing to the reaction. Understanding these emotions enables couples to navigate disagreements with empathy and compassion, fostering greater emotional intimacy and connection.

Recognizing Contributions to Conflict

Self-reflection also involves recognizing our contributions to conflicts within the marriage. It's easy to blame our partners for disagreements and misunderstandings, but the truth is that it often takes two to tango. By honestly assessing our role in conflicts, we can identify areas for personal growth and cultivate healthier patterns of interaction with our partners. For instance, if one partner tends to withdraw during disagreements, self-reflection may reveal underlying fears of confrontation or rejection. Acknowledging these patterns allows couples to work together towards more constructive conflict resolution strategies and strengthen their bond through mutual understanding and respect.

Personal Growth

Furthermore, self-reflection in marriage facilitates personal growth and development for both partners. It offers an opportunity to identify strengths, weaknesses, and areas for improvement, fostering a commitment to continuous learning and self-improvement within the relationship. Through self-reflection, individuals can gain clarity on their values, priorities, and long-term goals, aligning their actions with the shared vision for their marriage. Additionally, by reflecting on past experiences and challenges, couples can cultivate resilience, adaptability, and a more profound sense of connection as they navigate life's ups and downs together.

Ultimately, Self-reflection is a powerful tool that can help couples deepen their understanding of each other and build a stronger, healthier relationship. This can lead to greater compassion and less conflict, which is beneficial for both partners.

The Role of Self-Awareness in Marriage

Self-awareness plays a crucial role in a successful marriage. It helps you understand your thoughts, feelings, and actions and how they can impact your partner. This awareness helps you identify and manage your emotions, enabling you to communicate more effectively with your spouse.

When you are self-aware, you can better recognize your own patterns of behavior and how they may contribute to any issues in your marriage. For instance, if you tend to become defensive when your partner criticizes you, being self-aware can help you recognize this tendency and work on responding more calmly and constructively. Moreover, being self-aware enables you to understand your partner better. You can recognize when they are upset or struggling and respond in a compassionate and supportive way. It also allows you to communicate more effectively with your partner, as you can express your needs and desires in a way they can understand. Here are other vital roles self-awareness plays in Marriage:

Understanding Your Needs

Self-awareness enables individuals to identify and articulate their needs within the marriage. When you understand your emotions and needs well, it becomes easier to communicate your feelings to your partner. This, in turn, helps your partner better understand you and your needs, which can lead to a more fulfilling and satisfying relationship.

Emotional Regulation

Self-awareness empowers individuals to manage their emotions effectively, especially during challenging or stressful situations within the marriage. When you are aware of your emotions, you can take steps to control them, which helps you avoid overreacting or responding inappropriately to your partner's actions. This can be particularly helpful during conflicts or stressful situations, where emotions can easily get out of control. It can also promote healthier communication and reduce the likelihood of escalating tensions within the relationship.

Taking Responsibility

Self-awareness involves taking ownership of one's thoughts, feelings, and actions within the marriage. It allows individuals to recognize their role in conflicts or misunderstandings and take responsibility for their contributions to the situation. Taking responsibility for your mistakes shows your partner that you are willing to own up to your shortcomings and work on improving yourself. This can help build trust and respect in your relationship.

Empathy and Compassion

Self-awareness fosters empathy and compassion toward yourself and your partner. When you understand your partner's vulnerabilities and insecurities, you can empathize more deeply with their experiences and perspectives. This creates a supportive and nurturing environment where both partners feel understood, valued, and validated in their emotions and experiences.

Cultivating Resilience

Self-awareness promotes resilience within the marriage, allowing individuals to navigate challenges and setbacks with strength and perseverance. Resilience enables you to bounce back from difficult situations and challenges, which is crucial when facing the inevitable ups and downs of married life. When both partners are resilient, they can work together to overcome obstacles and build a stronger, more resilient relationship, emerging stronger and more united in their commitment to each other.

Practical Steps for Enhancing Self-Reflection and Self-Awareness in Marriage

- **Practice Mindfulness:** Engage in mindfulness exercises as a couple to cultivate self-awareness and presence in the moment. This could include meditation, deep breathing exercises, or simply walking together and observing your surroundings. Mindfulness practices can help you become more attuned to your emotions and reactions in real time. This can be particularly helpful during conflicts or stressful situations.
- **Seek Feedback:** Encourage open and honest communication by actively seeking feedback from your partner about your behaviors, communication style, and how you impact the relationship. Be receptive to constructive criticism and use it as an opportunity for

growth and self-improvement. This can provide valuable insights and help you understand yourself from another perspective.

- **Engage in Personal Development:** Attend workshops and seminars, read books, or take online courses focusing on personal development. This will help you gain new insights into yourself and your relationships. You'll also learn new skills to help you become a better partner in your marriage.
- **Set Personal Goals:** Take some time to think about what you want to achieve in your personal and professional life. Whether working on your communication skills, managing anger, or becoming more empathetic, personal growth benefits you and your marriage. Write down your goals and make a plan to achieve them.
- **Schedule Regular Check-Ins:** Set aside dedicated time with your partner to reflect on your relationship and individual experiences. This could be a weekly or monthly check-in where you discuss your thoughts,

feelings, and any challenges you may be facing. Use this time to practice active listening and empathy towards each other's perspectives.

By practicing these steps, you and your partner can enhance your self-reflection and self-awareness, leading to a happier and more fulfilling marriage.

Identifying Personal Values and Goals

Before getting married, it's crucial to have open and honest conversations about your personal values and goals. Personal values are the principles and beliefs that guide your behavior and decision-making. Identifying your values helps you understand what is truly important to you and what you want to prioritize in life.

Here are some tips and insights on how to go about this process:

- **Reflect on your own values and goals:** To start the process, take some time to reflect on your own values and goals. Think about what is important to you, what you value most, and what you hope to achieve in the short and long term. Once you clearly understand your values and goals, you can begin communicating them to your partner.
- **Communicate and listen to your partner:** Communication is key in any relationship, including marriage. Be open and honest with your partner about your values and goals. Share your thoughts, feelings, and aspirations respectfully and non-judgmentally. It's also important to listen to your partner's values and goals; understanding their perspective is just as important as expressing yours.
- **Find common ground and set mutual goals:** While you and your partner may have different values and goals,

it's crucial to find common ground and areas of overlap. Identify shared values and objectives that you prioritize and can work towards together. Once you better understand each other's values and goals, work together to set mutual goals for your marriage. These goals can be related to various aspects of your life, such as finances, family planning, career aspirations, personal growth, and more.

- **Revisit and reassess regularly:** Values and goals can evolve, so it's essential to revisit and reassess them regularly. Schedule check-ins with your partner to discuss how your values and goals may have changed and how you can continue to support each other in achieving them. If you and your partner have difficulty identifying or aligning your values and goals, consider seeking support from a couples therapist or counselor.

Emotional intelligence and communication skills

Emotional intelligence and communication skills are two essential elements for building and maintaining a healthy, happy, and successful marriage. Emotional intelligence refers to one's ability to recognize, understand, and regulate one's own emotions and those of one's partner. It involves being aware of one's emotional state and effectively expressing and managing one's emotions healthily. Developing emotional intelligence is fundamental for good communication in marriage.

Effective communication skills such as active listening, empathy, and assertiveness are crucial for a fulfilling marriage. They empower partners to express their needs and desires, understand each other's perspectives, and resolve conflicts respectfully and constructively. When both partners possess good communication skills, they can build a solid and healthy relationship based on mutual understanding, trust, and emotional connection.

Let's examine each of these elements individually to fully comprehend the significance of emotional intelligence and effective communication skills in the context of marriage.

Emotional Intelligence in Marriage

Emotional Intelligence in Marriage is essential for a successful relationship. To ensure a strong emotional connection in your relationship, here are some key elements that you should consider:

- **Self-awareness:** Knowing your emotions, triggers, and behaviors is important in a marriage. Understanding how you feel and why you feel that way can help you communicate more effectively with your partner.
- **Self-regulation:** Managing your emotions and reactions is crucial in preventing conflicts from escalating. Being able to control impulses and think before reacting can prevent unnecessary arguments.

- **Empathy:** Understanding and empathizing with your partner's emotions is crucial for building trust and a deeper connection. Seeing things from their perspective can help you respond more compassionately.
- **Social skills:** Effective communication, conflict resolution and collaboration are all important social skills necessary for a marriage. Building a strong emotional bond with your partner requires good social skills.

Communication Skills in Marriage

Communication is an essential aspect of a strong and successful marriage. Here are some tips to improve your communication skills with your partner:

- **Active Listening:** One of the most important skills is listening to your partner without interrupting or thinking about your response. This will help you understand each other better and gain a deeper understanding of your partner's perspective and needs.

- **Expressing Feelings:** Expressing your emotions in a constructive way using "I" statements instead of blaming language can prevent misunderstandings and conflicts.
- **Non-Verbal Communication:** Paying attention to non-verbal cues such as body language, tone of voice, and facial expressions can provide valuable insights into your partner's feelings.
- **Conflict Resolution:** Learning to resolve conflicts calmly and respectfully is crucial to effective communication. This helps avoid communication breakdowns and find mutually beneficial solutions, strengthening your relationship.
- **Assertiveness:** Both partners should assert their needs and boundaries while respecting each other. This leads to healthier communication patterns and a more balanced relationship.

In a healthy and happy marriage, communication skills and emotional intelligence are intertwined. Couples who can effectively communicate their emotions, needs, and concerns while empathizing with each other are more likely to build a strong, meaningful, and enduring relationship.

CHAPTER TWO

MINDFUL OR LUSTFUL UNION

MARRIAGE IS A COMPLEX and dynamic relationship that involves two individuals with different personalities, backgrounds, and desires. While many forces can either make or break a marriage, two fundamental forces that can have a significant impact are mindfulness and lust. While both are important, they can often conflict with each other, leading to superficial connections and a lack of emotional intimacy. Before taking your vows, it is essential to ask yourself whether you are in a mindful or purely lustful union. Your answer to this question can give you a good idea of your relationship's overall health and longevity. In a mindful union, couples prioritize open and honest communication, empathy, and understanding. They actively listen to each other, validate each other's experiences, and approach conflicts with compassion and curiosity rather than defensiveness or hostility. On the other hand, a lustful union is often characterized by intense physical attraction, but it may lack the emotional depth and commitment necessary for a lasting relationship.

While physical attraction is undoubtedly an essential aspect of any relationship, it is not enough to sustain a marriage over time. Couples who focus solely on physical attraction and sexual desire may feel unfulfilled and disconnected from each other. Conversely, couples mindful of each other's needs and feelings, communicate openly and honestly, and consciously deepen their emotional connection are more likely to build a strong, successful relationship. In this chapter, we will explore the concept of mindfulness and lust and their impact on the success of a marriage. We will examine the contrast between mindful and lustful union, the importance of cultivating a mindful connection, and strategies for balancing passion and mindfulness.

UNDERSTANDING MINDFULNESS AND LUST

What is a Mindful Union?

A mindful union is a marriage built on mutual respect, empathy, and understanding. Couples in a mindful union are committed to developing a deep emotional connection with each other and working together to build a meaningful life. In a mindful union, both partners are fully present and engaged, paying attention to each other's thoughts, emotions, and sensations without judgment or distraction. One of the key characteristics of a mindful union is emotional intimacy. Emotional intimacy is sharing one's thoughts, feelings, and vulnerabilities with another person without fear of judgment or rejection. Vulnerability is the willingness to be open and honest about one's thoughts, feelings, and insecurities, even if it means risking rejection or criticism. In a mindful union, both partners are open and honest with each other and communicate openly and empathetically. They are willing to listen to each other's perspectives, validate their emotions, and support each other through good times and bad.

In a mindful union, couples also work together to create shared experiences and memories that strengthen their bond. They engage in activities that they both enjoy, try new things together, and try to create meaningful moments that they can look back on with fondness and joy. Overall, a mindful union is a marriage characterized by emotional intimacy, vulnerability, and a strong commitment to each other. Couples in a mindful union work together to build a meaningful life. They are willing to put in the effort and commitment necessary to sustain their relationship. While a mindful union is not without its challenges, it is a type of marriage that can bring partners great joy, fulfillment, and happiness.

Exploring lustful union

In a marriage, physical attraction and desire, known as lust, can be a powerful force that brings excitement and passion to the relationship. It's normal to feel a strong desire for your partner, to want to be near them, to touch them, and to experience the rush of physical pleasure. However, it's important to understand that lust is only one aspect of a relationship and cannot sustain a healthy and long-lasting connection on its own.

A healthy marriage requires emotional intimacy, mutual respect, trust, and effective communication. While physical attraction is undoubtedly an essential element of a marriage, it should not be the only thing that matters. Couples who prioritize lust over emotional intimacy may find themselves in a shallow relationship that lacks depth and meaning. They may focus solely on physical pleasure and neglect their partner's emotional needs, leading to the marriage's breakdown.

It's essential to connect with your partner on a deeper level, to understand their needs, and to support them in their goals and aspirations. Couples who prioritize emotional intimacy and mindfulness in their marriage can still experience passion and desire for each other. In fact, a deep emotional connection can enhance physical intimacy and create a more fulfilling and satisfying relationship overall. It's important to note that lust is not inherently bad or negative in a marriage. In fact, physical attraction and desire can be an important part of a healthy relationship. However, it's essential to balance lust with emotional intimacy and commitment to ensure a strong and lasting union.

Contrasting mindfulness and lust

When thinking about marriage, we often associate it with romantic love and passion. As mentioned earlier, love is crucial to a successful marriage but not enough to build a lasting union. Mindful unions prioritize conscious decision-making and intentional commitment, offering a more sustainable and fulfilling partnership.

Understanding the difference between a mindful union and a lustful one is important. Lustful unions are primarily driven by physical attraction and infatuation, which can initially be intense and exciting. However, these relationships often lack the depth and emotional connection necessary for long-term stability. As the initial spark fades, couples may find it challenging to maintain the same level of passion and excitement, leading to dissatisfaction and potential dissolution of the marriage.

On the other hand, mindful unions are based on a deliberate choice to commit to one another, even when the initial infatuation fades. These unions are founded on shared values, mutual respect, and a deep understanding of each other's needs and desires. Couples in mindful unions practice conscious communication, active listening, and empathy towards each other, laying the foundation for a stable and fulfilling marriage that can withstand the test of time.

Balancing Passion and Mindfulness

Intimacy is an essential aspect of any healthy relationship. When it comes to intimacy, finding the right balance between physical desire and emotional connection can be challenging for many couples. However, it is possible to integrate passion and mindfulness in your relationship and strike a balance that works for both partners.

Passion is important in any intimate relationship, but it's not enough. Emotional connection is equally essential for building a strong and lasting bond. Couples who prioritize mindfulness and emotional connection often report higher levels of satisfaction and intimacy in their relationships.

So, what can couples do to balance passion and mindfulness? *Here are some tips:*

- **Communicate openly:** Talk to your partner about what you want and need from your physical and emotional relationship. This creates a safe space for both partners to express themselves authentically without fear of judgment.
- **Practice Mindful Awareness:** Being present in the moment during intimate interactions fosters a deeper emotional connection. Mindfulness techniques, such as deep breathing and focusing on sensations, can help couples enhance their connection and enjoyment of each other.
- **Prioritize Emotional Connection:** While physical desire is important, prioritizing emotional connection builds trust, intimacy, and a deeper bond between partners. Engaging in meaningful conversations, sharing vulnerabilities, and actively listening to each other strengthens emotional connection.

- **Explore Sensuality:** Sensuality encompasses a wide range of experiences beyond sexual intercourse. Couples can explore sensuality through activities such as sensual massages, cuddling, and engaging in shared hobbies that evoke pleasure and connection.
- **Make time for intimacy:** Set aside time for physical intimacy and emotional intimacy. Schedule regular date nights or other activities that allow you to connect emotionally.
- **Embrace Spontaneity:** While routines can be comforting, embracing spontaneity in the relationship keeps things exciting and fosters passion. Surprising each other with small gestures of affection or spontaneous romantic gestures can reignite the spark between partners.

CHAPTER THREE

COMPATIBILITY AND SHARED VALUES

WHEN IT COMES TO marriage, compatibility is one of the most important factors to consider. To ensure a successful and fulfilling marriage, it's essential to have a deep understanding of your partner's beliefs, values, and goals. Compatibility allows couples to communicate effectively, compromise when needed, and support each other through life's ups and downs. In my experience, despite that I loved my husband from the beginning, we lacked compatibility in many areas. We didn't share similar interests, values, and beliefs, which made it hard for us to work towards achieving things together. Furthermore, my husband's did not take our incompatibility serious which often led him to suppress my dreams. I felt voiceless and unheard, as effective communication was lacking in our marriage. This feeling can be overwhelming and heartbreaking, no matter how strong you are.

While it's true that no two people can be exactly alike, it's essential to make sure that your partner's differences are manageable and don't cause too much conflict. It's crucial to be open to compromise and work together to solve any issues. When you're compatible, you build a strong foundation of trust, respect, and love, the building blocks of a successful marriage. Compatibility is a crucial factor in a successful marriage. So, if you're considering marriage, take your time to get to know your partner and ensure that you're truly compatible. With the right mindset and a willingness to work together, you can build a happy and fulfilling life together.

Shared Values and Beliefs

To have a successful and fulfilling marriage, partners must share the same values and beliefs. This creates a solid foundation for a couple to build a happy life together. When partners prioritize important values such as honesty, loyalty, trust, and communication, they are more likely to build a strong and meaningful relationship. Similarly, shared beliefs, such as religion, politics, and family values, help partners have a common vision for their future together. This alignment of core values and beliefs can also help couples navigate difficult times and overcome challenges together. Conversely, when couples have conflicting values and beliefs, finding common ground and working together effectively can be difficult.

Importance of having aligned core values and beliefs in a marriage

Having aligned core values and beliefs in a marriage is important for several reasons:

- **Foundation for Compatibility:** Firstly, it is a crucial foundation for compatibility between partners. When individuals have similar beliefs, priorities, and life goals, it creates a strong bond and sense of alignment within the relationship, making understanding each other's perspectives and motivations easier.
- **Enhanced Communication:** Aligned core values also facilitate effective communication between partners, leading to more transparent communication and fewer misunderstandings. When couples share common values, they can better understand each other's viewpoints and resolve conflicts respectfully and constructively.
- **Conflict Resolution:** Having shared values provides a framework for resolving conflicts and differences of

opinion. Couples who share core values are better equipped to find compromise and work through disagreements and are more likely to work together to find a solution when faced with challenges.

- **Mutual Support and Encouragement:** Shared values create a sense of solidarity and mutual support within the marriage. When partners are aligned in their beliefs and goals, they can encourage and uplift each other, fostering a sense of teamwork and partnership.
- **Stability and Security:** Aligning core values in a marriage promotes stability and security for both partners. When individuals feel that their values are respected and validated within the relationship, they experience greater trust and emotional security, strengthening their bond.
- **Coherence in Decision-Making:** Shared values provide clarity and coherence in decision-making processes within the marriage. Couples can confidently make

important life decisions when a common set of values and principles guides them.

Identifying Common Goals

Identifying common aspirations and life objectives can bring you and your partner closer and create unity within your relationship. It allows you to work towards the same things and support each other in achieving your dreams. Having shared goals can also help you avoid potential conflicts or disagreements.

If you both have a clear understanding of what you want to achieve together, you'll be less likely to get sidetracked by individual goals that may conflict with each other. Of course, it's important to remember that you and your partner are individuals with unique aspirations and goals. It's okay if you don't share every goal with your partner, but it's crucial to find a balance between individual and shared goals.

When identifying common goals in a marriage, here are some key points to consider:

- **Open Communication:** Both partners should openly discuss their aspirations, dreams, and priorities to identify areas of overlap and shared interests.
- **Shared Values and Beliefs:** Couples should reflect on their shared values and consider how to translate them into tangible goals they both strive towards.
- **Long-term Vision:** Couples should also establish a long-term vision for their marriage and future together. This could include goals related to career, family, finances, personal development, and lifestyle preferences.
- **Compromise and Flexibility:** It's essential to recognize that each person brings their unique perspective and priorities to the relationship and finding common ground may require some negotiation and adjustment.
- **Prioritization:** Not all goals are equally important, and couples may need to prioritize their common goals based on their significance and feasibility. Identifying

the most important goals can help couples effectively focus their energy and resources.

- **SMART Goals:** Setting SMART (Specific, Measurable, Achievable, Relevant, Time-bound) goals can help couples create clear and actionable objectives. Breaking down larger goals into smaller, manageable tasks can make them more attainable and provide a sense of progress.
- **Regular Review and Evaluation:** Goals may evolve as circumstances change and priorities shift. Couples should regularly review and evaluate their common goals to remain aligned with their shared vision and values.
- **Celebrating Milestones:** Celebrating milestones and achievements can strengthen the bond between partners and motivate them to continue working towards their common goals. Acknowledging progress and success reinforces the sense of partnership and collaboration within the marriage.

Emotional Compatibility

Emotional compatibility is a crucial component of a successful and fulfilling marriage. It refers to the ability of two partners to understand, express, and manage their emotions and those of each other.

Emotional compatibility is essential to building a deep, lasting, passionate connection with your partner. To be emotionally compatible, you must possess emotional intelligence, empathy, and the ability to provide support. These qualities will allow you to build a relationship based on mutual respect and understanding.

Emotional intelligence

Emotional intelligence is an essential ingredient of emotional compatibility. It involves understanding, expressing, and managing emotions in oneself and one's partner. When both partners possess high emotional intelligence, they are better equipped to handle conflicts and communicate effectively.

Understanding emotions is the foundation of emotional intelligence. It involves being aware of one's own emotions and the emotions of others. This understanding allows individuals to empathize with their partner's feelings and perspectives, leading to more effective communication and problem-solving. Expressing emotions is also an essential aspect of emotional intelligence. Effective communication involves being able to express oneself clearly and respectfully while listening actively to one's partner. In a healthy relationship, both partners should feel comfortable expressing their emotions without fear of judgment or criticism.

Managing emotions is the final aspect of emotional intelligence. It involves being able to regulate one's own emotions and respond appropriately to the emotions of one's partner. This means avoiding destructive behaviors like yelling or name-calling and instead practicing healthy coping mechanisms like taking a break to cool down or seeking support from a trusted friend or therapist.

Empathy and support

Empathy and support are also vital components of emotional compatibility. Empathy is the ability to put yourself in your partner's shoes and understand their perspective. Empathy allows you to connect with your partner more deeply and fosters greater emotional intimacy. Support, on the other hand, involves being there for your partner when they need you most. Support can take many forms, such as offering a listening ear, providing encouragement, or simply being physically present.

Empathy and support are essential for building a strong emotional foundation in a marriage. When partners feel understood and supported by one another, they are more likely to feel secure and confident in their relationship. This sense of security and confidence can help couples weather the inevitable storms of married life. It's important to note that emotional compatibility isn't something that happens automatically. Like any other aspect of a marriage, emotional compatibility requires effort and attention. Couples must be willing to communicate openly and honestly about their emotions and needs. They must also be willing to listen actively and empathetically to their partner's concerns.

Tips for Building Stronger Emotional Compatibility

If you're looking to build stronger emotional compatibility in your marriage, consider the following tips:

- **Practice active listening.** This means giving your partner your full attention when speaking and trying to understand their perspective.
- **Express your emotions honestly and openly.** Don't be afraid to share your feelings with your partner, even if they are difficult or uncomfortable.

- **Practice empathy.** Put yourself in your partner's shoes and try to understand their perspective. This can help you connect more deeply and emotionally with your partner.
- **Offer support when your partner needs it.** This can be as simple as offering a listening ear or providing a shoulder to cry on.
- **Work on building your emotional intelligence.** This can involve reading books, taking courses on emotional intelligence, or simply practicing mindfulness and self-reflection.

CHAPTER FOUR

THE PSYCHOLOGICAL ASPECT OF RELATIONSHIPS

HAVE YOU EVER NOTICED THAT your thoughts and behaviors in romantic relationships tend to follow a particular pattern? Perhaps you feel uneasy about being alone for too long or feel confident and trustful with your partner. One explanation for these patterns is attachment theory. It's a psychological, evolutionary, and ethological theory that explores human connections, particularly between a caregiver and an infant. The theory proposes that how a child bonds with their caregiver during their early years shapes their expectations and behaviors in future relationships. Knowing your unique attachment style can help you become more self-aware and establish healthier long-term partnerships.

Understanding Attachment Theory

Attachment Theory is an interesting psychological framework that British psychologist John Bowlby developed in the 1950s. It focuses on the emotional bond between individuals, particularly between children and their main caregivers (e.g., parents, grandparents, etc.). The theory suggests that early experiences significantly impact adult relationships and emotional well-being. The core of attachment theory is the bond between infants and their caregivers. This bond is vital for the child's emotional development, as it provides a secure base from which they can explore the world and develop a sense of trust and security.

According to Attachment Theory, early attachment experiences shape our beliefs about ourselves, others, and the world. This creates an internal working model of self and others that influences our relationships in adulthood. If our early attachment experiences were positive and secure, we develop a secure working model of self and others, which allows us to form secure relationships in adulthood. However, if our early attachment experiences were negative or insecure, we develop an insecure working model of self and others, which can lead to the formation of insecure relationships in adulthood.

Attachment Styles

There are four main attachment styles: secure, anxious-preoccupied, dismissive-avoidant, and fearful-avoidant. These styles significantly influence how you perceive and respond to intimacy, trust, and emotional closeness. It's crucial to note that compatibility in relationships can stem from having compatible attachment styles or from partners understanding and working with each other's attachment needs. Therefore, exploring your attachment style and understanding how it may impact your interactions with others if you want to build a healthy and fulfilling relationship is worthwhile. So, let's delve into each of these attachment styles individually.

1. Secure Attachment Style:

A secure attachment style is characterized by a strong sense of trust and comfort with emotional intimacy. People with this attachment style have a positive view of themselves and others, feel comfortable with intimacy, and seek close relationships. They effectively communicate their needs, trust their partners, and are responsive to their partner's needs. They can give and receive support and feel secure in their relationships.

2. Anxious-Preoccupied Attachment Style

Individuals with an anxious-preoccupied attachment style tend to have a negative view of themselves but a positive view of others. They desire close relationships but often worry about rejection or abandonment. They may exhibit clingy or needy behaviors, constantly seek reassurance, and have difficulty trusting their partner's love and commitment.

3. Dismissive-Avoidant Attachment Style

People with a dismissive-avoidant attachment style usually have a positive view of themselves but a negative view of others. They value independence and self-reliance, often preferring autonomy over intimacy. They may avoid emotional vulnerability and downplay the importance of relationships. They may appear emotionally distant, have difficulty expressing or recognizing their own emotions, and may prioritize personal goals over relationships.

4. **Fearful-Avoidant Attachment Style**

Individuals with a fearful-avoidant attachment style typically have a negative view of both themselves and others. They may have experienced inconsistent caregiving or traumatic experiences in early life, leading to a fear of intimacy and a desire for closeness simultaneously. They may struggle with trust, manage emotions, and alternate between seeking and avoiding relationships. Understanding your attachment style can significantly impact your adult relationships. It can help you identify recurring patterns in your relationships and work towards building stronger connections with the people around you. This can lead to healthier and more fulfilling connections with others.

What is your attachment style?

Identifying your attachment style can be challenging as it requires a great deal of self-reflection and examination of your own actions and experiences in close relationships. If you find it difficult to answer this question accurately, don't worry; you are not alone. However, understanding your attachment style can be valuable in improving and enhancing your relationships.

To identify your attachment style, you must take a step back and examine your actions and experiences in close relationships. Do you seek emotional intimacy and closeness, or do you prefer to maintain a sense of independence and avoid emotional vulnerability? Do you feel anxious or fearful when your partner is unavailable, or do you feel comfortable giving each other space? Reflecting on these questions and considering how your behaviors align with the different attachment styles can provide insight into your own attachment style.

Developing a secure attachment style

It is possible to develop a secure attachment style even if you have a negative one. The process requires you to engage in self-reflection and make a conscious effort to change. It may be challenging, especially if you have had difficult or traumatic experiences in the past. However, with the right mindset and approach, it is achievable. Here are several strategies you can use to cultivate a more secure attachment style:

- **Identify your attachment style:** The first step in developing a secure attachment style is to identify your current attachment style. Are you anxious, avoidant, or secure in your relationships? Understanding your attachment style will help you recognize patterns in your behavior and identify areas for improvement.
- **Practice self-awareness:** Self-awareness is key to developing a secure attachment style. Take time to reflect on your emotions and reactions to different

situations. Ask yourself why you feel a certain way and how your behavior might impact your relationships.

- **Communicate effectively:** Effective communication is critical in building secure attachments. Be open and honest with your partner and express your thoughts and feelings clearly. Listen actively and try to understand your partner's perspective.
- **Build trust:** Trust is essential in developing a secure attachment style. Be reliable, consistent, and follow through on your commitments. Show your partner that you are dependable and can be counted on.
- **Address past traumas:** Past traumas can impact your attachment style. If you have experienced trauma in the past, seek professional help to address it. Healing from past wounds will allow you to form healthy attachments in the future.
- **Practice self-care:** Taking care of yourself is critical in developing a secure attachment style. Make time for self-care activities that bring you joy and relaxation. Feeling

happy and fulfilled makes you more likely to form healthy attachments with others.

- **Seek therapy:** It can be helpful to seek out professional support or guidance, particularly if you have experienced trauma or difficult past experiences that are impacting your relationships. Therapy or counseling can provide a safe and supportive environment to explore your attachment style and work towards building healthier, more fulfilling relationships.

Attachment Wounds and Healing

We all carry emotional wounds from our past experiences and traumas in our life journey. These wounds shape our personality, behavior, and the way we interact with others in our present lives. Attachment wounds are one of the most significant emotional injuries affecting our relationship dynamics. Recognizing attachment wounds is essential in understanding and addressing the underlying issues that may impact relationship dynamics.

Some common signs of attachment wounds include difficulty trusting others, fear of abandonment, feeling unworthy of love, and an inability to express emotions. These wounds can manifest in various ways, from being overly clingy in relationships to avoiding them altogether.

What are Attachment Wounds?

Attachment wounds are emotional injuries that occur in our early life due to the absence of a secure attachment figure, neglect, abandonment, abuse, or other traumatic experiences. These wounds can affect our emotional regulation, self-esteem, and ability to form secure relationships in adulthood.

Types of Attachment Wounds

Attachment wounds can be categorized into four main types based on the kind of attachment style they create:

- **Anxious Attachment Wounds:** This type of wound occurs when the caregiver is inconsistent or unpredictable in responding to the child's needs. As a result, the child develops an anxious attachment style characterized by a fear of abandonment, clinginess, and a constant need for reassurance.
- **Avoidant Attachment Wounds:** This type of wound occurs when the caregiver is emotionally distant, neglectful, or rejecting towards the child. As a result, the child develops an avoidant attachment style characterized by emotional detachment, self-reliance, and a reluctance to form close relationships.
- **Disorganized Attachment Wounds:** This type of wound occurs when the caregiver is abusive or neglectful towards the child, creating a sense of fear and confusion

in the child. As a result, the child develops a disorganized attachment style characterized by anxious and avoidant behaviors, including dissociation, emotional deregulations, and difficulty trusting others.

- **Ambivalent Attachment Wounds:** This type of wound occurs when the caregiver is inconsistent in their responses to the child's needs, creating a sense of unpredictability in the child. As a result, the child develops an ambivalent attachment style, characterized by a constant need for attention and reassurance and anger and frustration when their needs are unmet.

Healing Attachment Wounds

Healing attachment wounds requires a combination of self-awareness, therapy, and healthy relationship experiences. It is possible to heal attachment wounds and develop secure attachment in adulthood, but it requires time, effort, and a willingness to confront difficult emotions. Here are some steps you can take to heal attachment wounds:

- **Develop Self-Awareness:** The first step in healing attachment wounds is to become aware of your attachment style and how it affects your relationships. Self-awareness can help you identify patterns of behavior and emotions that are rooted in your attachment wounds.
- **Seek Therapy:** Therapy can help you process and heal from past traumas and develop healthy coping mechanisms. A therapist can help you identify your attachment wounds and work through them in a safe, supportive environment.
- **Practice Mindfulness:** Mindfulness can help you regulate your emotions and develop a sense of inner calm. It can also help you become more aware of your thoughts, feelings, and behaviors, allowing you to make conscious choices that support your healing process.

- **Build Healthy Relationships:** Building healthy relationships with supportive, empathetic people can help you develop secure attachments in adulthood. Surround yourself with people who respect your boundaries, listen to your needs, and offer support when needed.

It is worth noting that although attachment styles, personality traits, and early life experiences can provide some insights into compatibility, they are not the sole determinants of a marriage's success or failure.

Relationships are complex, and various factors can influence compatibility. Essential components for building and maintaining a healthy and fulfilling partnership include effective communication, mutual respect, shared values, and ongoing effort.

Love Languages

Love languages are another psychological aspect of relationships that can significantly impact how partners perceive and express love. Understanding how you and your partner like to give and receive love is one of the most important aspects of any relationship, and the concept of love languages can help you with that. The idea of love languages was developed by Dr. Gary Chapman, a marriage counselor and author of "The Five Love Languages: How to Express Heartfelt Commitment to Your Mate." According to Chapman, there are five primary love languages: words of affirmation, acts of service, gift-giving, quality time, and physical touch.

1. Words of Affirmation

Words of affirmation are powerful love language that can significantly impact your partner's overall well-being and happiness. This love language is all about using words to express love, appreciation, and encouragement. It can be as simple as saying "I love you" or as specific as pointing out something your partner did that you appreciate. If your partner's primary love language is words of affirmation, they may feel most loved when you express your feelings through verbal expressions.

This could involve complimenting their appearance, acknowledging their accomplishments, or simply telling them how much they mean to you. However, words of affirmation should be genuine and heartfelt. Empty compliments or insincere praise can come across as disingenuous and may even backfire. Instead, focus on being specific and authentic in your expressions of love and appreciation. Here are some examples of words of affirmation that you can use to express love to your partner:

- "I'm so grateful for you."
- "You make me so happy."
- "I love the way you always make me laugh."
- "You're so talented and capable."

- "I appreciate all that you do for me."

To truly connect with your partner through words of affirmation, focus on being specific and authentic in your expressions of love and appreciation. Take the time to think about what you appreciate about your partner and how you can put those feelings into words. When you express yourself genuinely and heartfelt, your partner will feel seen, heard, and loved.

2. Acts of Service

Acts of service are a form of love language that makes your partner feel loved and appreciated. It involves demonstrating love and support by performing thoughtful gestures and helpful tasks. If your partner's primary love language is acts of service, they may feel most loved when you go out of your way to make their life easier. Acts of service can range from doing simple chores like the dishes to taking care of a task that your partner has been putting off. They should be done without expecting anything in return, out of love and a genuine desire to support your partner. Here are some examples of acts of service that you can do to show love to your partner:

- Cook a meal for your partner
- Clean the house or apartment
- Do the laundry
- Take care of the kids or pets
- Run errands for your partner
- Help your partner with a project

Acts of service should be done willingly, without prompting, and without expecting anything in return. If your partner has to ask you to do something, it may have a different impact than if you had done it on your own.

3. Gift-giving

Gift-giving is another love language that can make your partner feel loved and appreciated. This love language involves choosing meaningful gifts that resonate with your partner's interests, preferences, and love language. If your partner's primary love language is gift-giving, they may feel most loved when you surprise them with a thoughtful and meaningful present. It's important to note that gift-giving doesn't have to be expensive or extravagant. What matters most is the thought and effort you put into choosing the gift. When selecting a gift, consider your partner's interests, hobbies, and preferences. Think about what would make them happy and what they would appreciate. Here are some examples of thoughtful gifts that you can give your partner to show your love:

- A book by their favorite author
- A piece of jewelry that holds sentimental value
- A personalized photo album or scrapbook
- A thoughtful card or letter expressing your feelings
- A surprise date night or weekend getaway
- A homemade gift, such as a knitted scarf or baked goods

The secret to effective giving is to focus on the thought and effort behind the gift rather than the cost. Every gift is priceless, regardless of its cost. The value of a gift lies in the thought, love, and effort behind it, not in the price tag. Even a simple and inexpensive gift can be incredibly meaningful if it's chosen with care and given with love.

4. Quality Time

Quality time is a love language that involves spending meaningful time with your partner. If your partner's primary love language is quality time, they may feel most loved when you give them your undivided attention and focus on building a deeper connection.

Quality time can involve doing activities together, such as walking, watching a movie, or simply having a meaningful conversation. It's important to note that quality time should be intentional and focused on building a stronger relationship. This means putting away distractions like phones or computers and actively engaging in the moment with your partner. Here are some examples of quality time activities that you can do with your partner:

- Take a weekend trip together
- Have a game night or movie night
- Go for a hike or bike ride together
- Have a meaningful conversation over dinner
- Plan a surprise date or outing
- Attend a class or workshop together

These activities can help you to build a stronger bond with your partner and show them that you care about them. Quality time is not just about spending time together; it's also about being present and engaged at the moment with your partner.

5. Physical Touch

Physical touch is another love language that can make your partner feel loved and appreciated. It's all about using physical touch to express love and affection for your partner. If your significant other's primary love language is physical touch, then they may feel most loved when you show your affection through hugs, kisses, and other forms of physical touch.

However, physical touch should always be consensual and respectful. This means that you should always ask your partner for permission before initiating physical touch and be mindful of their comfort level. Here are some examples of physical touch that you can use to show your affection to your partner:

- Give your partner a hug or kiss
- Hold hands while walking or sitting together
- Give your partner a massage or foot rub
- Snuggle on the couch while watching a movie
- Playfully touch your partner's arm or shoulder
- Show your affection through gentle touches or caresses

As much as this is a beautiful and powerful way to express love and affection for your partner if your partner doesn't feel comfortable with it, you should respect their wishes and find other ways to show your love and appreciation.

How to Receive and Express Love

To determine your love language and your partner's, Chapman suggests paying attention to how you and your partner express love. Do you prefer to give gifts or receive compliments? Do you enjoy spending quality time with your partner or receiving physical affection? Once you understand your love language and your partner's, you can work to express love in ways that resonate with both of you.

How to Receive Love

- **Know Your Love Language:** Understanding your own love language is the first step in receiving love effectively. Reflect on what makes you feel most loved and communicate this to your partner.

- **Communicate Your Needs:** Clearly communicate your love language to your partner. Express what actions or gestures make you feel loved and appreciated, helping them understand how to fulfill your emotional needs.
- **Acknowledge Efforts:** When your partner expresses love in your preferred love language, acknowledge and appreciate their efforts. This positive reinforcement encourages continued expression of love in ways that resonate with you.
- **Be Open and Receptive:** Remain open to receiving love in different ways, even if they're not your primary love language. Recognize and appreciate the intent behind your partner's actions, fostering a sense of connection and closeness.

How to Express Love

- **Learn Your Partner's Love Language:** Pay attention to how your partner expresses love and what actions or words make them feel most loved. Understanding their love language allows you to tailor your expressions of love accordingly.
- **Show Consistency:** Consistency is key to expressing love effectively. Make an effort to consistently speak your partner's love language, demonstrating your love and care through actions and words that resonate with them.
- **Be Thoughtful:** Thoughtfulness goes a long way in expressing love. Take the time to plan thoughtful gestures or surprises that align with your partner's love language, showing that you pay attention to their emotional needs.
- **Listen and Respond:** Listen actively to your partner's needs and desires, and respond with love and

understanding. Show empathy and support, making them feel valued and cherished in the relationship.

Understanding and speaking your partner's love language is a powerful tool for building a solid and healthy relationship. So take the time to learn your love language and your partner's, and try to express love in those ways. You'll be amazed at its positive impact on your relationship.

CHAPTER FIVE

RELATIONSHIP RED FLAGS AND BEHAVIOR PATTERN

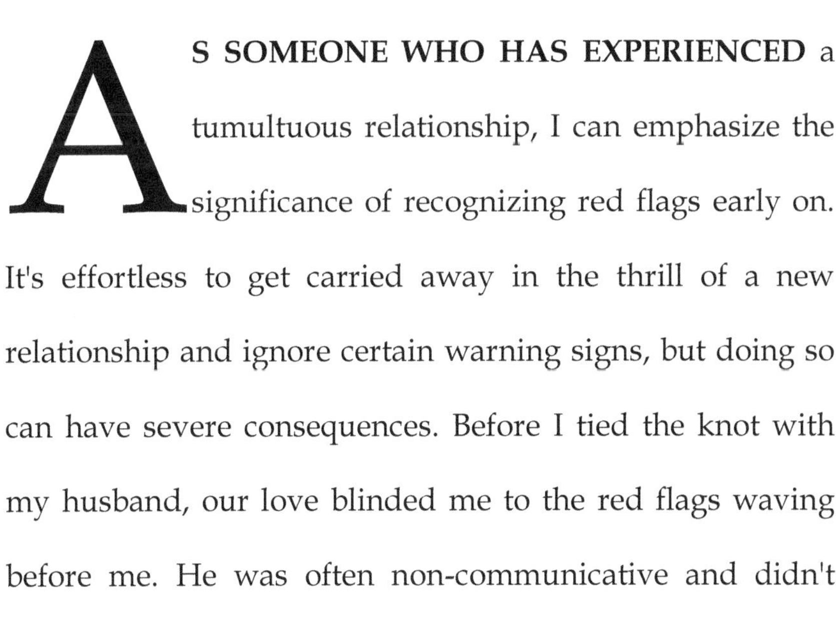

AS SOMEONE WHO HAS EXPERIENCED a tumultuous relationship, I can emphasize the significance of recognizing red flags early on. It's effortless to get carried away in the thrill of a new relationship and ignore certain warning signs, but doing so can have severe consequences. Before I tied the knot with my husband, our love blinded me to the red flags waving before me. He was often non-communicative and didn't share his goals or aspirations with me. He was also very competitive and always put himself and maternal family first. We had minimal shared values and beliefs among many other things. Have you heard the saying? When a person shows you who they are "Believe them" but we rather make excuses for them. Seriously, believe them. But despite these warning signs, I convinced myself he would change over time, and I stayed in the relationship.

Even as we married, I overlooked these red flags, convincing myself that love could conquer all. I believed that if I tried harder to be the perfect spouse, those red flags would disappear. However, as time passed, the red flags only multiplied, becoming glaring reminders of the reality I had chosen to ignore.

His temper, his dismissive attitude towards my aspirations, and his belief that my role was solely to fulfill traditional expectations of a wife became unbearable. Yet, I clung to the hope that things would improve, refusing to acknowledge the inevitable truth. Eventually, I reached a breaking point. I realized that staying in the marriage would only erode my health, sanity and peace of mind further. Leaving was the only option for my well-being, a decision that came with immense pain and regret for ignoring the red flags from the start.

Looking back, I wish I had paid more attention to the warning signs before I tied the knot. If I had done so, I could have avoided the many years of unhappiness in my marriage and the heartache that came with the breakup. Instead, I learned that ignoring red flags is never a good idea. Don't make the same mistake I made; don't brush aside red flags in hopes of a brighter future. Instead, confront them head-on, communicate openly with your partner, and assess whether the issues are surmountable. If the red flags persist and compromise your happiness and stability, have the courage to walk away. It's better to prevent a broken home than to endure the consequences of ignoring warning signs.

Early Warning Signs

When starting a new relationship, it's easy to get swept up in the excitement and overlook potential issues that may arise in the future. However, paying attention to early warning signs that indicate a partner's character and behavior could become problematic is essential. By recognizing these red flags early on, we can make informed decisions about whether or not to continue the relationship.

Identifying Red Flags

There are certain behaviors and attitudes that may indicate potential issues in a relationship. These can include:

- **Controlling behavior:** If a partner tries to control your actions, restrict who you spend time with, or make decisions for you without your input, it's a red flag. Control is unhealthy in any relationship, and it can be a sign of deeper issues, such as insecurity or a need for power.

- **Lack of communication:** Communication is key in any relationship, and if a partner is unwilling or unable to communicate effectively, it can lead to misunderstandings and frustration. If a partner constantly avoids difficult conversations or shuts down when you try to discuss issues, it's a warning sign.
- **Dishonesty:** Honesty is the foundation of any healthy relationship, and lying about important matters such as finances, past relationships, or personal issues is a major red flag. Trust is also essential in a relationship; without it, the foundation crumbles.
- **Lack of empathy:** Empathy is understanding and sharing another person's feelings. If a partner consistently disregards your feelings, dismisses your concerns, or shows a lack of empathy toward others, it's a warning sign. A lack of empathy can lead to a one-sided relationship where one partner's needs are consistently ignored.

- **Manipulation:** Manipulation can take many forms, from subtle guilt-tripping to more overt tactics such as gas lighting or emotional blackmail. If a partner consistently tries to manipulate you into doing things you don't want to do or makes you feel guilty for setting boundaries, it's a major red flag.

Trust Your Instincts

When assessing a partner's character, it's essential to pay attention to your gut feelings and intuition. If something feels off or doesn't sit right with you, it's worth exploring further. Our instincts are often our first line of defense when it comes to potential danger or issues, so it's important to trust them.

Examples of Red Flags

Here are some specific examples of behaviors that may warrant attention in a relationship:

- Your partner constantly cancels plans at the last minute or doesn't show up when they say they will.
- Your partner makes you feel guilty for spending time with friends or family.
- Your partner constantly criticizes or belittles you in private or in front of others.
- Your partner is overly jealous or possessive.
- Your partner refuses to take responsibility for their actions or blames others for their mistakes.
- Your partner constantly avoids discussing essential topics or shuts down when you try to have a conversation.
- Your partner has a history of cheating or infidelity.

Patterns of Behavior

Behavior patterns can reveal a lot about a person's character and intentions. When it comes to marriage, paying close attention to your partner's actions and behaviors is crucial.

Observing consistency, paying attention to actions, and noticing inconsistencies are three essential skills that can help you assess your partner's character and build a healthy, long-lasting relationship.

1. Observing Consistency

Consistency is a vital indicator of a person's character. People who exhibit consistent behavior patterns are likely to be trustworthy, reliable, and have a strong sense of integrity. Consistency means that a person's actions align with their values and beliefs, making them honest, transparent, and open with others. To observe consistency, you must observe your partner's behavior over time and in different situations and contexts. For example, if your partner constantly treats you respectfully, communicates effectively, and tries to support your goals and dreams, it strongly indicates that they are dependable and trustworthy. This will make you feel confident in the strength of your relationship.

2. Paying Attention to Actions

Actions speak louder than words. While words can be persuasive, they can also be misleading. People who are not genuine or honest can use words to manipulate and deceive others. Therefore, focusing on a person's actions is important to determine their true character. You need to observe your partner's actions over time to determine if they are true to their word and if they follow through on their commitments. For example, if your partner constantly helps with household chores and shares responsibilities, it shows their dedication and commitment to the relationship.

3. Noticing Inconsistencies

Inconsistencies or discrepancies in a person's behavior can be red flags that indicate they are not trustworthy or dependable. For example, if your partner is attentive and loving one day and then distant and uninterested the next, this could indicate that they are not fully committed to the relationship. It is important to recognize and address these inconsistencies before they become bigger issues. Noticing inconsistencies can help you identify when someone is lying or hiding something from you. It can also help you better understand your partner's needs, desires, and emotions, leading to improved communication and a stronger relationship. To notice inconsistencies, you must be observant and attentive to details.

Core Character Assessment

When assessing someone's character and evaluating their potential for a meaningful relationship, take a deeper look at their core values, integrity, and empathy. These three aspects are the foundation of a person's character and can give you a good indication of whether or not they are a good fit for you.

1. Understanding Core Values

Core values are the fundamental beliefs and principles that guide a person's actions and decisions. These values may be shaped by various factors, such as upbringing, education, and life experiences. By exploring a person's core values, you can gain insight into what motivates them and what they prioritize in life. For example, if family is a core value for someone, you can expect that they will prioritize spending time with loved ones and value close relationships. Understanding a person's core values is crucial because it helps you determine whether your values align with theirs. If your values and principles don't align, it may lead to conflicts and misunderstandings in the future.

2. Assessing Integrity

Assessing a person's integrity is another critical aspect of determining their character. Integrity refers to a person's honesty, ethics, and moral principles. Someone with strong integrity will be truthful, reliable, and consistent in their actions and words. On the other hand, someone who lacks integrity may be deceitful, manipulative, or untrustworthy. Assessing your partner's integrity will help determine whether you can trust them. If they lack integrity, they may be more likely to deceive you, which could lead to negative consequences.

3. Evaluating Empathy and Compassion

Empathy and compassion are critical components of a person's character. Empathy is the ability to understand and share the feelings of others, while compassion is the desire to alleviate their suffering. Someone empathetic and compassionate will be able to connect with others on a deeper level and will be more likely to prioritize the needs of others. This can be especially important in a romantic relationship, where empathy and compassion are essential for building trust and intimacy. Evaluating a person's capacity for empathy and compassion helps you determine whether they can form meaningful relationships. If someone lacks empathy and compassion, they may struggle to connect with others emotionally, leading to difficulties in building and maintaining relationships.

Addressing Red Flags

When we identify certain negative patterns or red flags in our partner's behavior, it's important to address them promptly. Ignoring these red flags in a relationship can lead to bigger problems in the future, such as misunderstandings, arguments, resentment, and even breakups. Therefore, it's crucial to tackle these issues head-on. Here are some strategies to address and resolve relationship problems that stem from red flags to avoid future complications.

1. Acknowledge the red flags

The first step in addressing relationship issues stemming from red flags is acknowledging they exist. This may involve having a difficult conversation with your partner, but it's vital to be honest and transparent about your concerns. You can start by saying, "I've noticed that we've been arguing a lot lately, and I think there are some underlying issues that we need to address. Can we talk about it?"

2. Identify the root cause

Once you've acknowledged the red flags, identify the root cause of the issue. This may involve digging deeper to uncover underlying emotions or behavior patterns contributing to the problem. For example, if you're arguing about money, it may be that one or both of you have different attitudes toward spending and saving. By identifying the root cause of the problem, you can work towards finding a solution that addresses the underlying issue.

3. Communicate effectively

Effective communication is key to resolving relationship issues stemming from red flags. This means listening actively, expressing yourself clearly, and being open to feedback. Avoid blame and criticism and instead focus on finding solutions that work for both of you. Communicating effectively can build trust and intimacy in your relationship and work towards a more positive future together.

4. Seek help if necessary

Sometimes, resolving relationship issues stemming from red flags may require outside help. This could involve seeking the advice of a couples therapist or relationship coach. These professionals can provide tools and techniques to help you work through your issues and offer objective feedback to help you see things differently.

CHAPTER SIX

SUPERFICIAL, DEEP AND SPIRITUAL CONNECTIONS

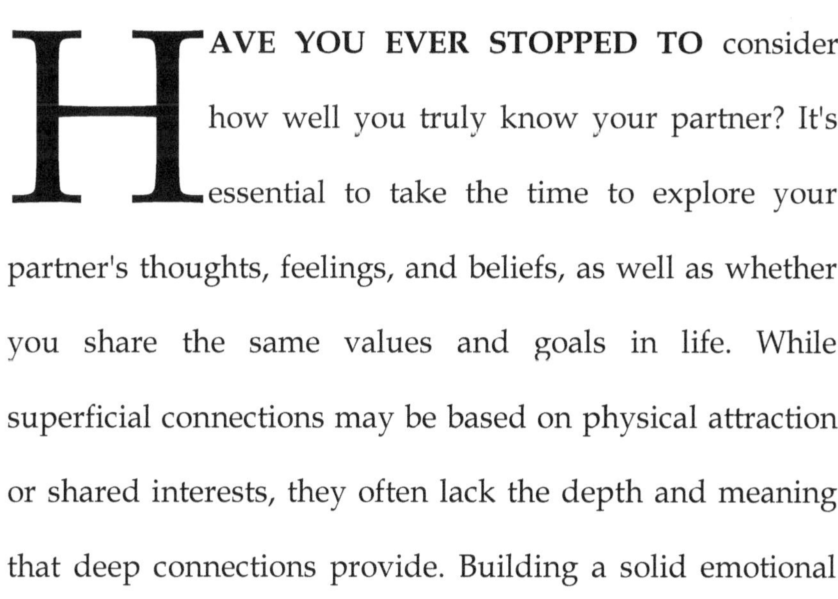

HAVE YOU EVER STOPPED TO consider how well you truly know your partner? It's essential to take the time to explore your partner's thoughts, feelings, and beliefs, as well as whether you share the same values and goals in life. While superficial connections may be based on physical attraction or shared interests, they often lack the depth and meaning that deep connections provide. Building a solid emotional bond through a deeper understanding of each other's inner world is the key to forming deep connections. Furthermore, spiritual connections involve a shared sense of purpose and a connection to something greater than yourselves. Recognizing and understanding these different levels of connection is essential for building and maintaining healthy relationships that stand the test of time.

Superficial Love

Superficial love is primarily based on surface-level interactions, typically characterized by physical attraction, shared interests, and everyday experiences. However, such relationships often lack emotional depth and intimacy, as they are formed based on external factors rather than a deeper understanding of the person. Superficial connections may also be based on shallow criteria, such as looks, status, or material possessions, rather than genuine connection and shared values. For instance, you may find someone attractive based on their physical appearance or enjoy their company because of shared interests. While these factors can be substantial, enjoyable, and provide a sense of belonging, they are often short-lived and do not lead to deeper connections.

Characteristics of superficial connections may include:

- **Physical Attraction:** Relationships based solely on physical attraction prioritize appearance over deeper emotional connection or compatibility.
- **Shared Interests:** While shared interests can be a positive aspect of a relationship, superficial connections may rely heavily on superficial hobbies or activities without delving into deeper values or beliefs.
- **Surface-Level Interactions:** Superficial connections may involve shallow conversations that avoid topics of substance or vulnerability. Discussions revolve around

superficial topics such as pop culture, gossip, or material possessions.

- **Lack of Emotional Intimacy:** Emotional intimacy, vulnerability, and trust are often lacking in superficial connections. Partners may avoid sharing their thoughts and feelings, preferring to maintain a façade of perfection or detachment.

Impact of Superficial Connections on Relationships

Superficial connections can significantly impact our relationships. When we prioritize superficial connections over meaningful ones, our ability to form deep and lasting bonds is limited. In some cases, superficial connections can even prevent us from realizing the value of genuine connections with others. Over time, this reliance on superficial connections can lead us to become disconnected from our authentic selves and core values. Superficial relationships have several limitations in fostering meaningful and lasting connections; they include:

- **Shallow Foundation:** Relationships built on superficial connections lack a strong foundation of emotional intimacy and mutual understanding. As a result, they are more susceptible to dissolution when faced with challenges or conflicts.
- **Lack of Depth:** Superficial connections often fail to address deeper emotional needs and desires, leading to a sense of emptiness or dissatisfaction in the relationship.
- **Short-lived and Fickle:** Superficial love can be fleeting and easily influenced by external circumstances. It may not withstand challenges or difficulties, as the foundation of the relationship is not strong.
- **Inauthenticity:** Partners may feel pressured to maintain appearances or conform to societal expectations rather than being their authentic selves. This can lead to

feelings of alienation and disconnection within the relationship.

- **Difficulty in Resolving Conflict:** Without a strong emotional bond, couples in superficial relationships may struggle to communicate and resolve conflicts effectively. Issues may be ignored or swept under the rug rather than addressed constructively.
- **Emotionally Unsatisfying:** Individuals in a superficial relationship may feel emotionally unfulfilled or disconnected, as the focus is more on the surface-level aspects rather than on deeper emotional bonds.

Recognizing Superficiality in Relationships

It can be challenging to recognize signs of superficiality in our relationships, as these connections can often feel enjoyable and comfortable at the moment. However, some key indicators can help us identify when our relationships lack depth and emotional intimacy.

Signs of superficiality may include:

- **Focus on External Appearance:** One of the most obvious signs is focusing on external appearance or material possessions over emotional connection or compatibility. This means that partners prioritize physical appearance or the things that they have rather than forming a deep emotional connection.
- **Lack of emotional connection:** Superficial connections often revolve around shared interests or experiences rather than our more profound thoughts and feelings. If you find yourself constantly engaging in small talk or surface-level conversations with someone, it may indicate that your relationship lacks the emotional depth needed to foster a meaningful connection.
- **Lack of Depth in Conversations:** This could be a red flag if your conversations with your partner revolve around superficial topics such as the weather or the

latest celebrity gossip and avoid discussions of deeper emotions or values.

- **Avoidance of Vulnerability:** Superficial connections can often feel safe and comfortable, but they can also prevent us from sharing our true selves with others. If you find yourself holding back or avoiding conversations that require vulnerability and emotional openness, it may indicate that your relationship is lacking in depth.
- **Short-Term Gratification:** If your relationship primarily focuses on immediate gratification or pleasure rather than long-term growth and fulfillment, this could be a sign that you're not connecting on a deeper level. Similarly, if your partner is only interested in spending time with you when it's convenient for them or when they want something from you, this could be a sign that the relationship lacks mutual respect and care.
- **Constantly seeking validation:** If you continually seek validation or approval from your partner, it may be a

sign that your relationships are superficial. Meaningful relationships are built on mutual respect and acceptance rather than external validation or approval.

If you're concerned that your relationship might be superficial, it's essential to take the time to reflect on your values and priorities and to communicate openly and honestly with your partner about your needs and expectations. It's possible to cultivate fulfilling and meaningful relationships with effort and commitment.

Deep Love

Deep love is a rare and precious thing. It is not just about physical attraction or fleeting infatuation but rather a strong emotional connection that goes beyond superficiality. Deep love is about truly knowing and understanding someone, accepting their flaws and imperfections, and being there for them through thick and thin. It requires vulnerability, trust, and willingness to maintain the relationship. If you're lucky enough to find someone who loves you deeply and unconditionally, hold onto them tightly and cherish every moment together. Some additional attributes of deep connections may include:

- **Trust:** A deep connection is built on a foundation of trust, where both parties feel secure in the relationship and confident in each other's intentions.
- **Communication:** Clear and open communication is essential in deep connections, allowing for honest expressions of thoughts and feelings.
- **Support:** In deep connections, both parties provide emotional support and encouragement to each other, even in difficult times.
- **Understanding**: A deep connection involves understanding the other person's needs, desires, and motivations.

Benefits of deep connections in relationships

- **Increased happiness:** Studies have shown that people with deep connections report higher happiness and satisfaction.
- **Better mental health:** Strong connections have been linked to better mental health outcomes, including lower rates of depression and anxiety.
- **Improved physical health:** Deep connections have also been associated with better physical health outcomes, such as lower blood pressure and improved immune function.
- **Greater fulfillment:** Deep connections provide a sense of purpose and meaning, which can lead to greater fulfillment and satisfaction in life.

Nurturing Deep Connections

Nurturing deep connections requires effort and intentionality. It involves getting to know someone on a deeper level and being vulnerable enough to share your thoughts, feelings, and experiences. While some people may naturally gravitate towards deep connections, it may take more effort and intentionality for others. Here are a few strategies for nurturing deep connections in relationships:

- **Be present:** Deep connections require presence and attention. When spending time with someone, put away distractions and focus on being fully present.
- **Be Authentic:** Be true to yourself, and don't be afraid to express your thoughts and feelings. Authenticity is critical to building deeper connections.
- **Practice active listening:** It is important to actively listen to your partner during communication. This means avoiding interrupting or judging and showing that you understand and value their thoughts and feelings.
- **Be Vulnerable:** Vulnerability can be scary, but it's essential to building deeper connections. Share your thoughts and feelings with your partner and be open to receiving their thoughts and feelings in return.

- **Show empathy:** Understanding and empathy go hand in hand. When the other person shares their feelings, try to understand their perspective and show compassion towards their experience.
- **Cultivate shared experiences:** Shared experiences are a powerful way to build connections and create lasting memories. Make an effort to do things together that you both enjoy and that align with your shared values. It could be anything from trying a new activity together to traveling to a new place.
- **Celebrate Differences:** Differences can bring us closer together if we embrace them. Celebrate your partner's unique qualities and perspectives, and be open to learning from them.

Spiritual Love

Spiritual love is a kind of love that I have recently experienced. This love is profound and goes beyond all other forms of love. It is not based on physical attraction or emotional attachment but on a deep connection that exists at the spiritual level. It is a type of love that our creator has inspired us to feel and share with others. This love is unconditional, selfless, and pure.

When we love someone spiritually, we are able to see beyond their physical appearance and flaws. We connect with their soul, their innermost being and appreciate them for who they truly are. We recognize their values, beliefs, and their connection to something greater than themselves. This enables us to love them for their true essence rather than what they do or say. Here are some key aspects of spiritual love relationships:

- **Deep Connection:** Spiritual love is often characterized by a deep connection at the soul level. Partners feel like they have known each other for eternity and share a profound understanding of each other.

- **Unconditional Love**: Spiritual love is often associated with unconditional love, where partners accept each other fully and support each other through all ups and downs without judgment.
- **Shared Values:** Partners in a spiritually loving relationship often share core values and beliefs that strengthen their connection and help them navigate life's challenges together.
- **Growth and Transformation:** Spiritual love in relationships can be transformative, pushing both partners to grow, evolve, and become the best versions of themselves.
- **Purpose and Meaning**: Couples who experience spiritual love often feel a sense of purpose and meaning in their relationship, believing they are meant to be together for a higher reason.

- **Connection to Something Greater:** Spiritual love can also involve a connection to something greater than the individual partnership, such as a higher power, the universe, or a shared spiritual practice.
- **Emotional and Energetic Bond:** Partners in a spiritually loving relationship may feel a strong emotional and energetic bond that transcends the physical realm, leading to a sense of oneness and unity.

Cultivating Spiritual Connections

Cultivating spiritual connections with a partner requires effort and commitment. It involves exploring and understanding each other's beliefs and values and finding ways to deepen your connection through shared experiences. Here are some ways to cultivate spiritual connections with your partner:

- **Share your beliefs and values:** Take the time to discuss your individual beliefs and values with your partner.

This can help you both understand each other better and find common ground.

- **Practice mindfulness together:** Mindfulness involves being present and paying attention to your thoughts and feelings. Practicing mindfulness together can help you deepen your connection and improve your communication.
- **Attend spiritual events:** Attending spiritual events such as religious services, meditation classes, or yoga retreats can provide opportunities for you and your partner to connect on a deeper level.
- **Support each other's spiritual growth:** Encourage your partner to explore their spirituality and support them in their journey. This can help you both grow individually and as a couple.

It's crucial to understand that spiritual love is a deeply personal and subjective experience that can manifest differently for different couples. Some couples may find a spiritual connection through shared religious beliefs, while others may experience it through a deep emotional and energetic bond.

Balancing Superficial, Deep, and Spiritual Love Connections

To have a fulfilling love life, it's essential to maintain a balance of Superficial, Deep, and Spiritual Connections, as an imbalance can lead to problems. For instance, a purely superficial relationship may lack emotional depth and intimacy, while a relationship that is too spiritual may lack passion and physical intimacy. **So, how can we balance these connections?** Here are some strategies that can help you achieve this balance:

- **Self-Reflection:** Take time to consider your needs and preferences in a relationship. Are you prioritizing one type of connection over the others? Understanding your desires and motivations can help you strive for balance.

- **Open Communication:** Communicate openly and honestly with your partner about your needs and preferences. Discuss what superficial, deep, and spiritual connections mean to both of you and how you can support each other in cultivating them.
- **Quality Time Together:** Dedicate quality time to nurturing each connection in your relationship. Make time for lighthearted activities that foster superficial connections, such as having fun dates or engaging in shared hobbies. Similarly, prioritize deep conversations that promote emotional intimacy and understanding and explore spiritual practices together that deepen your connection on a soul level.
- **Balance of Activities:** Strive for a balance of activities catering to each connection type. Mix in playful and enjoyable experiences for superficial connections, meaningful conversations, shared experiences for deep connections, and spiritual practices that align with your beliefs and values.

- **Embrace Vulnerability:** Allow yourself and your partner to be vulnerable in these areas. Share your thoughts, feelings, and desires openly, even if they feel uncomfortable or challenging. Vulnerability fosters intimacy and strengthens all types of connections in a relationship.
- **Mutual Respect and Understanding:** Respect each other's preferences and boundaries regarding superficial, deep, and spiritual connections. Avoid judgment or pressure to conform to a particular ideal and appreciate the unique qualities that each connection brings to your relationship.
- **Flexibility and Adaptability:** Be flexible and willing to adapt to changes in your relationship dynamics over time. As your relationship evolves, your needs and desires in these areas may also change. Stay open to exploring new experiences and adjusting your approach accordingly.

CHAPTER SEVEN

DIFFERENTIATING INFATUATION FROM DELUSION

WHEN IT COMES TO ONE OF the most significant decisions of our lives, such as choosing a life partner, it is crucial to clearly understand our feelings and emotions. Sometimes, we may confuse infatuation or delusion with genuine attraction, which can cloud our judgment and lead to regrettable consequences. Infatuation can be short-lived and may fade over time, making us wonder why we were so attracted to someone initially. On the other hand, delusion is a much more serious issue that can have long-lasting consequences. Before tying the knot, it is essential to take a step back and evaluate your feelings. Are you genuinely attracted to this person, or are you just infatuated with them? Are you seeing them clearly, or are you deluding yourself about who they are and what your relationship is really like?

Answering these questions honestly can help you make decisions based on reality rather than just your emotions. To better understand the differences between infatuation and delusion, let's delve into what each means individually and what sets them apart.

Understanding Infatuation

Infatuation is a powerful and all-consuming attraction that combines idealization, obsession, and physical attraction toward another person. It is typically a temporary experience that lasts from a few weeks to several months. Although it can make people feel like they are on cloud nine, infatuation can also cause them to lose touch with reality and make poor decisions. This intense emotional state is often characterized by overwhelming passion, obsession, and a strong desire to be with someone. However, it is important to remember that infatuation is temporary and can fade over time.

Let me illustrate this with an example. Mark's heart skipped a beat as Nichole walked into the crowded room. Her graceful figure caught his eye, and he couldn't look away. Every move she made seemed to captivate him, and her every word sounded like music to his ears. Consumed by her presence, he found himself daydreaming about her, imagining a future where they were together, where her laughter filled his days, and her touch ignited his senses. He felt a magnetic pull towards her that he couldn't resist despite barely knowing her. He was infatuated, blinded by her beauty and charm, unable to see any flaws. Although his friends warned him to be cautious, he brushed off their concerns, convinced that what he felt was true love. However, as he spent more time with her and got to know her better, he began to see her imperfections and the cracks in the facade. As a result, the infatuation gradually faded, giving way to a deeper and more meaningful understanding of who she was. Mark could see the reality of Nichole's true self. If he didn't connect with her beyond the infatuation, their relationship would likely end alongside the infatuation. However, if Mark connected with Nichole on a deeper level, a seed was planted that would eventually grow into something deeper and more meaningful - love.

Infatuation and True Love

Infatuation and true love are two distinct stages of romantic feelings. Infatuation is characterized by intense passion, excitement, and attraction toward someone, but it is frequently based on idealized perceptions and physical chemistry rather than a deep emotional connection. On the other hand, true love involves a more profound bond, genuine care, understanding, and commitment toward the other person. True love is not just about being infatuated with someone's appearance or charm. It's about connecting with them deeper, accepting their flaws, and being willing to grow together. Although infatuation could eventually evolve into true love, it usually requires more than feelings to develop into something lasting and beautiful. Time, patience, and effort are crucial in nurturing and strengthening relationships to build a solid foundation of true love.

Time plays a significant role in a relationship's growth. As time passes, partners can get to know each other on a deeper level, understand each other's values, beliefs, and quirks, and create shared experiences that contribute to developing a meaningful connection. Patience is essential in cultivating true love because relationships go through ups and downs, challenges, and conflicts that require understanding, compromise, and forgiveness. Patience allows partners to weather difficult times together, work through differences, and grow stronger as a couple. Lastly, work is vital in transforming infatuation into true love. Building a healthy and fulfilling relationship takes effort, communication, and mutual respect. It involves actively listening, showing empathy, being supportive, and prioritizing the relationship in both partners' lives.

Signs of Infatuation

Infatuation can manifest itself in various ways, and several signs indicate that someone is experiencing it. Some common signs of infatuation include:

- **Obsessive thinking:** Infatuation often leads people to think about the other person constantly, obsessing over every detail of their life and behavior.

- **Excessive idealization:** Infatuation can cause people to see the other person as perfect without flaws or faults. This idealization can be unrealistic and make it difficult for people to see the other person as they are.
- **Physical attraction:** Infatuation is often accompanied by strong physical attraction, intense desire, and longing.
- **Emotional intensity:** Infatuation can produce intense emotions, including euphoria, excitement, and joy, as well as anxiety, nervousness, and insecurity.
- **Irrational behavior:** Infatuation can cause people to act irrationally, such as stalking others, making impulsive decisions, or ignoring red flags or warning signs.

Impact of Infatuation on Relationships

Infatuation can significantly impact relationships, affecting decision-making, perception, and emotional well-being. Some common effects of infatuation on relationships include:

- **Impaired decision-making:** Infatuation can impair people's ability to make rational decisions, leading them to make impulsive or ill-advised choices.
- **Perception distortion:** Infatuation can lead people to see others distortedly, idealizing them and ignoring any flaws or faults they may have.
- **Emotional instability:** Infatuation can produce intense emotions, including euphoria, excitement, and joy, as well as anxiety, nervousness, and insecurity, which can lead to emotional instability.
- **Short-lived:** Infatuation is a temporary experience that often fades, leaving people disillusioned and disappointed.

Lack of genuine connection: Infatuation is often based on physical attraction and idealization rather than a deep, meaningful connection with the other person.

Delusion: The Distorted Reality

Delusion is a mental state that goes beyond infatuation and involves a distorted perception of reality, which can cause significant distress and impair daily life. In a relationship, delusions can manifest in various ways, such as one partner having unrealistic expectations of the other or believing false information or interpretations about the relationship. Delusional partners may cling to their beliefs even when presented with evidence to the contrary, leading to negative consequences for their relationships.

Jealousy or paranoia can also take the form of delusions, with one partner imagining scenarios that are not based on reality and becoming overly possessive or suspicious of the other. This can also involve one partner making assumptions about the other's thoughts or intentions without factual evidence, leading to misunderstandings and conflicts.

For instance, let's consider a scenario where Samantha and John have been in a relationship for a few months. Samantha has a history of being cheated on by her previous partners, which has caused her to develop trust issues. Despite John's reassurances and consistent behavior, Samantha doubts his faithfulness. She starts to imagine scenarios in her head, such as John being interested in another woman at work or flirting with someone online. She becomes increasingly paranoid and starts to check John's phone and social media accounts for any evidence of infidelity. On the other hand, John is entirely faithful and feels hurt and frustrated by Samantha's lack of trust. He tries to reassure her and show her that he is committed to their relationship, but Samantha's delusions persist.

This scenario illustrates how delusions can cause significant harm to a relationship, even if they are not based in reality. It is essential to address these delusions in a relationship to prevent unhealthy dynamics and ultimately harm the relationship. This can be done through open communication, seeking the help of a therapist or counselor, and working together to establish realistic expectations and boundaries.

Signs of delusion

Here are several signs that may indicate delusion:

- **Denial:** Delusional individuals may deny that their beliefs are irrational, even when presented with evidence to the contrary.
- **Distortion of facts:** Delusional individuals may twist or distort facts to fit their beliefs. For example, they may interpret a friendly gesture as a hostile one.
- **Refusal to acknowledge evidence:** Delusional individuals may reject evidence contradicting their beliefs, even if a trusted source presents it.
- **Paranoia:** Delusional individuals may be paranoid, believing that others are out to get them or that they are being monitored.

- **Grandiosity:** Delusional individuals may have an inflated sense of self-importance, believing they have special powers or abilities.
- **Mood swings:** Delusional individuals may experience mood swings, ranging from elation to depression.

Impact on relationships

Delusion can significantly impact relationships, particularly those that are close and intimate. The following are some of the ways in which delusion can affect relationships:

- **Communication:** Delusional individuals may have difficulty communicating effectively with others, mainly if their beliefs are not based on reality. This can lead to misunderstandings, arguments, and a communication breakdown.
- **Trust:** Delusional individuals may have difficulty trusting others, especially if their beliefs involve

paranoia or a belief that others are out to get them. This can lead to a breakdown in trust, with delusional individuals becoming increasingly isolated and withdrawn.

- **Relationship dynamics:** Delusional individuals may become increasingly difficult to live with as their beliefs become more entrenched and their behavior becomes more erratic. This can lead to a breakdown in the relationship, with the delusional individual becoming increasingly isolated and alone.

Differentiating Infatuation from Delusion

Infatuation and delusion are two concepts that are often confused in relationships. While these concepts may share similarities, they differ in intensity, duration, and objectivity. Recognizing these differences can help us make informed decisions about our relationships and avoid getting caught up in unrealistic or harmful beliefs and behaviors. Infatuation is a natural part of the early stages of a relationship. It is characterized by strong feelings of attraction, desire, and excitement toward the other person. However, it is often temporary and can fade over time. On the other hand, delusion can be dangerous, as it is characterized by a belief or perception that is not based on reality. This can lead to staying in an unhealthy or abusive relationship and ignoring one's own needs and desires.

To differentiate between infatuation and delusion, take a step back and objectively evaluate your feelings and perceptions. Evaluate whether your feelings are based on an idealized version of your partner or if they are rooted in reality. Look for warning signs and red flags in the relationship, and don't ignore them just because you are infatuated with your partner. Finally, honest communication with your partner is key to any healthy relationship. It can help you avoid falling into the trap of delusion.

CHAPTER EIGHT

COMMUNICATION AND CONFLICT RESOLUTION

HAVE YOU EVER EXPERIENCED a situation where you struggle to communicate your desires and needs to your partner? If so, you're not alone. I've been there too. I vividly recall a time in my marriage when effective communication seemed impossible. My husband and I faced a significant hurdle because our conversations lacked depth and understanding. Despite my efforts to express my feelings and concerns, it felt like I was talking to a wall. My husband wasn't approachable, making it challenging to share my thoughts openly. This lack of communication took a toll on our relationship, leading to unresolved issues and frustrations. It wasn't until I realized the importance of effective communication that I began to seek solutions.

Effective communication isn't just about talking; it's about truly listening and understanding each other's perspectives. It requires vulnerability from both partners and a willingness to engage in meaningful dialogue. Without it, conflicts can escalate, and relationships can suffer. But when communication flows seamlessly, it forms the foundation of a strong and lasting connection. Through open and honest communication, couples can address issues, express their needs, and grow together.

So, if you've ever struggled with communication in your relationship, know that you're not alone. With effort and understanding, you can overcome these challenges and build a healthier, more fulfilling relationship based on effective communication.

Effective Communication

Effective communication is an essential component of healthy and successful relationships. It's the foundation upon which a strong and lasting connection is built. When couples communicate effectively, they create an environment of trust, understanding, and respect. This goes beyond just talking to each other; it involves active listening, empathy, and genuine engagement.

In a relationship, effective communication means being able to express your thoughts, feelings and needs openly and honestly. It also means listening attentively to your partner, seeking to understand their perspective without judgment or interruption. This kind of communication fosters mutual respect and validation, strengthening the bond between partners. One key aspect of effective communication is empathy. It's about putting yourself in your partner's shoes and understanding their emotions and experiences. When you approach conversations with empathy, you create a safe space for your partner to express themselves without fear of criticism or invalidation.

Another important element is assertiveness. Being assertive means expressing your thoughts and feelings confidently and respectfully. It's about speaking up for yourself, advocating for your needs, and considering your partner's needs. Assertive communication promotes honesty and transparency in a relationship, which is crucial for building trust and intimacy. Conflict resolution is also an integral part of effective communication. Disagreements and conflicts are inevitable in any relationship, but how couples handle them can make a big difference. Effective communication during conflicts involves active listening, validating each other's feelings, and working together to find mutually beneficial solutions. Furthermore, nonverbal communication plays a significant role in effective communication. Gestures, facial expressions, tone of voice, and body language can convey emotions and intentions more powerfully than words alone. Being aware of these nonverbal cues and responding to them appropriately can enhance understanding and connection in a relationship.

Effective communication in relationships is about creating an open, honest, and respectful dialogue between partners. It's about actively listening, empathizing, asserting, resolving conflicts constructively, and paying attention to nonverbal cues. When couples prioritize effective communication, they lay the groundwork for a strong, healthy, and fulfilling relationship.

Benefits of Effective Communication

Effective communication in marriage or any relationship brings numerous benefits to health and longevity. Let's delve into some of these benefits comprehensively:

1. Enhanced Understanding

When partners communicate effectively, they gain a deeper understanding of each other's thoughts, feelings, and needs. This understanding strengthens the emotional connection and builds empathy, which is essential for maintaining intimacy and closeness.

2. Increased Trust

Effective communication promotes trust and transparency in a relationship. When partners feel comfortable expressing themselves without fear of judgment or criticism, trust naturally grows. This trust forms the foundation of a strong and secure bond, enabling couples to navigate challenges and conflicts confidently.

3. Conflict Resolution:

Effective communication enhances conflict resolution skills. Conflicts are inevitable in any relationship, but how they are managed can make a significant difference. When couples communicate effectively during conflicts, they listen actively, validate each other's feelings, and work towards finding solutions collaboratively. This leads to more constructive resolutions and strengthens the relationship in the long run.

4. Mutual respect and validation

Effective communication promotes mutual respect and validation. When partners actively listen to each other, acknowledge their feelings, and validate their experiences, they respect one another's perspectives. This validation builds a sense of mutual appreciation and fosters a supportive and nurturing environment within the relationship.

5. Reduced Misunderstandings

Effective communication reduces misunderstandings and miscommunications. Clear and concise communication helps prevent confusion and ensures that both partners are on the same page. This minimizes the likelihood of unnecessary conflicts or frustrations arising from misinterpretations.

6. Personal growth

Effective communication encourages personal growth and development within the relationship. When partners feel heard and understood, they are more likely to share their aspirations, goals, and concerns openly. This creates opportunities for mutual support and encouragement, empowering each partner to pursue their passions and ambitions while maintaining a strong connection with their significant other.

7. Healthy Boundaries:

Clear and open communication helps establish and maintain healthy boundaries within the relationship. Partners can express their needs and expectations, allowing for mutual respect and understanding of each other's boundaries. Ultimately, effective communication leads to greater overall satisfaction in the relationship. When partners feel heard, understood, and valued, they experience a deeper sense of fulfillment and happiness in their connection

Barriers to Communication

There are many barriers to effective communication in relationships. These include lack of trust, fear of rejection, and cultural differences. These include lack of trust, fear of rejection, and cultural differences. Other common barriers include;

- **Poor listening skills:** When partners are not fully present or attentive during conversations, they may miss important cues or fail to grasp the underlying emotions behind their partner's words. This can lead to misunderstandings and frustration, as one or both partners feels unheard or dismissed.
- **Defensiveness:** When individuals feel attacked or criticized during a conversation, they may become defensive and shut down, preventing meaningful dialogue. Defensiveness can escalate conflicts and create a hostile atmosphere, making it difficult to resolve issues constructively.
- **Lack of empathy:** Additionally, lack of empathy can hinder effective communication. If partners cannot empathize with each other's feelings and perspectives, they may struggle to connect emotionally and understand each other's experiences. This can lead to feelings of disconnect and isolation within the relationship.

- **Negative communication patterns:** Furthermore, negative communication patterns, such as criticism, contempt, defensiveness, and stonewalling, can undermine effective communication. These destructive behaviors can erode trust and intimacy, creating a toxic cycle of conflict and resentment within the relationship.
- **Unspoken expectations:** Moreover, unspoken expectations and assumptions can pose significant barriers to communication. When partners have different expectations or assumptions about roles, responsibilities, or behaviors, they may not effectively communicate their needs or desires, leading to misunderstandings and resentment.
- **Past issues:** Additionally, unresolved past issues or baggage from previous relationships can impact communication in the present. If partners bring unresolved emotional wounds or trust issues into the relationship, they may struggle to communicate

openly and authentically with each other, fearing vulnerability or rejection.

- **External stressors:** Furthermore, external stressors such as work pressures, financial difficulties, or family obligations can distract partners from engaging fully in communication. When individuals are overwhelmed or preoccupied with external concerns, they may lack the emotional bandwidth to communicate effectively with their partner.

Different Communication Styles

Effective communication is a crucial component of human interaction. We rely on communication to convey our thoughts, ideas, feelings, and emotions. However, not everyone communicates in the same way. Some people may exhibit assertive communication styles, while others might be more passive. Similarly, some individuals might display aggressive communication styles, while others may have passive-aggressive tendencies. In order to establish healthy relationships and prevent miscommunications, it's essential to understand the different communication styles.

1. Assertive Communication

Assertive communication is an incredibly valuable skill that can help to maintain healthy relationships. When you communicate assertively, you express yourself clearly and confidently while respecting the other person's feelings and needs. This kind of communication can be a powerful tool in relationships, allowing both partners to express themselves effectively and work together to resolve conflicts. Assertive communication helps you to express your needs and expectations clearly while being receptive to the other person's needs and expectations.

One crucial aspect of assertive communication is being direct and honest about your feelings and needs. This means expressing your thoughts and emotions from your perspective rather than blaming or attacking the other person. For instance, instead of saying, "You don't listen to me," you could say, "I feel frustrated when I don't feel heard."

Another essential aspect of assertive communication is being clear and explicit. This means expressing your needs and expectations straightforwardly rather than relying on hints or expecting the other person to read your mind. For example, instead of saying, "I wish you would spend more time with me," you could say, "I would like to spend more quality time with you."

When communicating assertively, it's also essential to be empathetic and practice active listening. This means giving your full attention and acknowledging the other person's feelings and needs, even if you don't agree with them. When listening, it's important to avoid interrupting or dismissing the other person's feelings and repeating what they've said to ensure that you've understood them correctly.

2. Passive Communication:

Passive communication is a communication style that can be detrimental to one's personal and professional relationships. It is often characterized by a reluctance to express one's thoughts, feelings, and needs. This communication style can lead to misunderstandings, unmet needs, and a lack of communication in a relationship. Passive individuals tend to prioritize the needs and preferences of others while neglecting their own, which can result in frustration and resentment.

In a relationship, passive communication can be harmful if it leads to a lack of communication. Passive individuals may avoid expressing their needs and feelings, causing their partners to feel disconnected and unsure how to support them. This communication style can also lead to a power imbalance in the relationship, where one partner is consistently prioritized over the other.

Passive communication can take many forms, including avoiding conflict, apologizing excessively, and failing to express emotions or opinions. Passive individuals may also use nonverbal cues, such as avoiding eye contact or slouching, to avoid expressing themselves. While passive communication can sometimes be an effective way to prevent conflict or maintain harmony in a relationship, it can also be detrimental if it leads to a lack of communication or unmet needs.

3. Aggressive Communication:

Aggressive communication is a style in which individuals prioritize their own needs and opinions over those of others. Such individuals often resort to using forceful and intimidating language to get their way, even if it means hurting or disrespecting others. This communication style is usually adopted by people who are frustrated, angry, or hurt, and they use aggressive communication to express their emotions. However, aggressive communication can be detrimental to relationships, as it can lead to feelings of fear, intimidation, and disrespect.

Aggressive communication can manifest in various forms in a relationship, including yelling, name-calling, blaming, or threatening. Aggressive individuals may also use physical gestures or behaviors, such as slamming doors or throwing objects, to intimidate others. Although aggressive communication may seem effective in getting what one wants in the short term, it can eventually damage relationships and cause feelings of hatred and mistrust.

The problem with aggressive communication is that it can lead to a breakdown in communication and can cause emotional and even physical harm to the people involved. When someone is on the receiving end of aggressive communication, they can feel attacked, intimidated, disrespected, devalued, and hurt. This can cause them to withdraw, become defensive, or shut down, making it difficult to resolve the issue. It can also cause the aggressive individual to feel isolated and unsupported, as others may avoid them due to their aggressive behavior.

4. Passive-Aggressive Communication:

Passive-aggressive communication is a style of communication that can be quite harmful to relationships. It involves expressing negative feelings, such as frustration or anger, in subtle and indirect ways. Unfortunately, this was the ideal type of communication that best described how my husband communicated. The problem with passive-aggressive communication is that it can make it difficult for the recipient to identify the problem's source, leading to misunderstandings, resentment, and mistrust. In a relationship, passive-aggressive communication can take many forms.

It may involve sarcasm, backhanded compliments, or even the silent treatment. Nonverbal cues like eye-rolling or sighing may also express negative feelings. While passive-aggressive communication may seem like a way to avoid conflict, it can ultimately damage relationships and lead to feelings of disconnection.

Passive-aggressive communication can negatively affect both parties in a relationship. It can cause the recipient to feel helpless, confused, and unsure how to respond. While the passive-aggressive individual may feel powerless and resentful, as their indirect communication may not effectively resolve their underlying issues.

If you want to establish healthy relationships, it is crucial to practice open and direct communication. If you realize that you tend to communicate passively, aggressively, or passive-aggressively, it would be beneficial to develop more assertive communication skills. This may involve being adaptable and flexible in your communication style and modifying it to suit the circumstances and the person you are communicating with. By doing so, you can prevent misunderstandings and strengthen your relationships.

Active Listening and Empathy

Active listening is an essential aspect of effective communication. It means paying close attention to what the other person is saying and showing that you understand their perspective. Active listening involves hearing the words and understanding the nonverbal cues and emotions behind them.

Active listening also involves showing empathy by putting yourself in the other person's shoes and understanding their feelings and experiences. You can achieve this by reflecting on what you've heard, asking clarifying questions, and validating your emotions. When you practice active listening and empathy, you can create a safe and supportive environment for open and honest communication. This, in turn, can lead to deeper connection and understanding in a relationship. Here are some ways you can practice active listening and empathy in your relationship:

Active Listening

- **Focus on the Speaker:** When you're actively listening, giving your spouse your undivided attention is crucial. This means eliminating distractions like phones, TVs, or other thoughts and genuinely focusing on your partner's words.
- **Paraphrase and Reflect:** Show that you are engaged by paraphrasing what your spouse has said in your own words. This demonstrates that you are actively listening and trying to understand their perspective.
- **Ask Clarifying Questions:** If something is unclear or you need more information, ask open-ended questions to delve deeper into what your partner is trying to communicate.
- **Validate Emotions:** Acknowledge and validate your spouse's feelings even if you don't necessarily agree with their perspective. Understanding their emotions can help strengthen your emotional connection.

- **Avoid Interrupting:** Let your partner finish speaking before you respond. Interrupting can signal that you are not genuinely listening or are more focused on your thoughts than their words.

Empathy

- **Put Yourself in Their Shoes:** To empathize with your spouse, imagine how they might feel in a particular situation and respond with sensitivity.
- **Show Understanding:** Show your partner that you understand their emotions using phrases like "I can see why you feel that way" or "I understand why this is important to you."
- **Offer Support:** Express empathy by offering support and reassurance to your spouse. Let them know that you are there for them and care about their well-being.
- **Be Non-Judgmental:** Avoid passing judgment on your partner's feelings or reactions. Everyone experiences

emotions differently, and creating a safe space for open communication without fear of criticism is crucial.

- **Practice Patience:** Cultivate patience in your interactions with your spouse. Empathy requires time and effort to understand your partner's perspective and emotions.

Conflict Resolution

Conflict is a natural part of human relationships. We all have different opinions, beliefs, and values; sometimes, these differences can lead to disagreements and conflicts. However, conflicts don't always have to result in harm and destruction. Instead, if managed effectively, they can be valuable opportunities for growth, learning, and mutual understanding.

To handle conflicts effectively, it's crucial to first comprehend the nature of conflict in relationships and its potential impact on communication and intimacy. This involves exploring the underlying causes of conflict, such as differences in expectations, needs, and communication styles. When you understand the root causes of conflict, you can more easily identify potential triggers and take steps to prevent conflicts from occurring.

When conflicts do arise, it's essential to approach them with a collaborative problem-solving mindset. This means framing conflicts as opportunities for growth and mutual understanding rather than as threats or sources of negativity. Collaborative problem-solving involves actively listening to the other person's perspective, expressing empathy and understanding, and working together to find a solution that meets both parties' needs.

Effective conflict resolution strategies

When it comes to managing conflicts, it is essential to use effective strategies that can help resolve them in a constructive manner. Techniques like active listening, compromise, and negotiation can be helpful in achieving this goal.

Active listening is a crucial skill that can help reduce tension and promote understanding between parties. It involves paying close attention to what the other person is saying, asking clarifying questions, and summarizing their perspective to ensure mutual understanding. Compromise is another helpful strategy for resolving conflicts by finding a middle ground that is acceptable to both parties. This involves identifying common ground and areas of agreement and then working together to find a solution that meets everyone's needs to some extent.

Negotiation is another powerful tool for resolving conflicts. It involves collaborating to find a mutually beneficial solution by identifying the needs and interests of both parties and working together to find a solution that meets those needs. During a negotiation, it is important to focus on the problem rather than the person and be open to exploring different options and possibilities.

Effective conflict resolution requires a willingness to listen, compromise, and negotiate. With the right strategies in place, conflict can be resolved constructively and promote positive relationships between parties.

Managing Emotions during Conflict

During moments of conflict, it's not uncommon for partners to say or do things that negatively impact each other's emotions. However, regulating these emotions can be the key to resolving the conflict healthily and productively. Emotional regulation involves learning to manage emotions effectively during conflicts to prevent escalation and promote resolution. This requires recognizing and acknowledging our emotions, identifying triggers, and taking steps to calm down when emotions escalate. It is crucial to be mindful of our words when we are in a heated argument with our partner because they cannot be taken back once they are out. It's okay to express ourselves, but we should avoid doing so in a disrespectful manner. If the argument becomes too heated, it's best to take a step back and understand our emotions before responding to our partner. This can be achieved by taking a few deep breaths, going for a walk, or engaging in another calming activity that allows us to process our feelings.

Once we better understand our emotions, we can communicate with our partners more constructively. This involves expressing our thoughts and feelings clearly and respectfully while also being open to listening to our partner's perspective.

CHAPTER NINE

FINANCES AND SHARED RESPONSIBILITIES

EVERY INDIVIDUAL'S RELATIONSHIP with money is unique and is shaped by their upbringing, experiences, and values. When two people come together in a relationship, they bring their individual perspectives, which may not always align perfectly. In my personal experience, my husband had a different approach to money than I did. He believed that throwing money at problems could solve anything, while I valued careful planning and saving for the future. One of the early signs of our financial incompatibility was our approach to shared responsibilities at home. While I diligently took on household chores and responsibilities, my husband were often absent or delegated tasks without actively participating. He didn't want to contribute to household duties… nor did he want to pay to get them done. However, it went beyond the money and was about shared responsibility. I felt he didn't care about our future and only thought about himself. Our differences in financial values and goals became more apparent as time passed. We had different life plans and couldn't find common ground on important decisions. While my husband pursued his military career, I was left to shoulder the burden of our family and business. I had my dreams, too, but my husband was only concerned about himself and never gave room for communication. Our lack of shared goals and values created a rift in our marriage, making it challenging to navigate our financial journey together and leading to constant tension and misunderstandings.

Having aligned values and goals with your partner is crucial for a healthy and successful marriage. It's essential to have open and honest communication about your beliefs and attitudes towards money. This includes discussing your attitudes towards debt, your approach to budgeting and saving, and your expectations regarding lifestyle and spending habits. If you and your partner have different financial values and goals, it can lead to conflict and resentment, as seen in my story. It's essential to find common ground and work towards shared goals rather than pursuing individual goals at the expense of the relationship.

Understanding Financial Compatibility

Financial compatibility is a crucial factor that often gets overlooked during the early stages of a romantic relationship. Taking the time to assess your financial compatibility with your partner before getting married is essential. It helps you to identify any potential areas of disagreement or conflict that may arise in the future. Studies have shown that financial incompatibility or disagreements are one of the leading causes of divorce. Therefore, it's crucial to establish financial compatibility early on in a relationship. This means discussing your financial past, present, and future and finding ways to compromise and collaborate on financial decisions. Failure to address these issues can lead to stress, tension, and even divorce. However, understanding each other's financial habits and goals can prevent these problems and build a solid foundation for a healthy financial future together. Let's explore some steps you can take to assess your financial compatibility as a couple.

Financial Values

Every person has their own unique set of financial values, which include their beliefs, attitudes, and priorities towards money management. These values serve as the basis for how you approach money in your marriage and guide all of your financial decisions. As a couple, they help you build a strong foundation for your financial journey together. Financial values encompass a wide range of preferences, such as a love for luxury, a dedication to education, a passion for travel, a desire for freedom and spontaneity, or a commitment to health and fitness. These values can reflect individual preferences, such as prioritizing experiences over material possessions, investing in personal and professional growth, valuing cultural exploration, embracing flexibility and enjoyment, or maintaining physical and mental well-being. They can also reflect shared values between partners, such as a commitment to charitable giving or a desire to save for a shared goal, like buying a home or starting a family.

These financial values not only shape how couples manage their finances together but also influence their overall lifestyle, goals, and aspirations within their marriage. Understanding your own financial values and those of your partner is crucial for building a solid financial foundation in your marriage and making decisions that align with your shared goals and priorities.

It's important to engage in meaningful conversations beyond income and expenses to gain a deeper understanding of each other's financial values. Ask questions like: What does money mean to you? How did your upbringing shape your money beliefs? What are your current financial priorities? How comfortable are you with taking on debt? You can build a strong and healthy financial future together by communicating honestly and openly about your financial values and working together to create a financial plan that reflects those values.

Financial Goals

Once you have a clear understanding of each other's values, it is essential to discuss your financial goals and ensure they are aligned. Your financial goals are the objectives you hope to achieve with your finances, both in the short-term and long-term. It is important to note that both short-term and long-term goals are vital in shaping your financial journey together.

Short-term goals are usually immediate financial priorities, such as saving for a vacation, paying off credit card debt, or building an emergency fund. On the other hand, long-term goals are significant milestones like purchasing a home, funding children's education, or securing a comfortable retirement. However, aligning these goals can be challenging, especially if both partners have different aspirations. For instance, if one partner is focused on saving for a down payment on a house while the other dreams of extensive travel, finding a middle ground becomes crucial. This may require both partners to compromise and devise creative solutions to balance both desires.

When discussing financial goals, be specific and realistic. Define concrete figures and timelines for achieving each goal, ensuring they resonate with both partners' values and aspirations. Regularly revisiting these goals allows for progress evaluation and adjustments as needed, ensuring your financial journey remains aligned with your shared vision for the future.

Financial Habits

Understanding how we handle our finances - our financial habits - is essential to building a strong and healthy relationship. It involves gaining insights into each other's spending patterns, saving behaviors, and attitudes toward debt. Each individual brings their own financial fingerprint to the table, which is a blend of their experiences and personal beliefs that influence their approach to money. Some people are natural savers, finding solace in building a secure financial future, while others derive pleasure from spending and cherishing the present moment and the enjoyment that comes with it. These underlying reasons for financial behavior are crucial to understand because they help us empathize with each other and work together towards shared goals. For instance, someone who grew up with financial struggles might be cautious with money as a way of feeling secure, whereas someone who had a more comfortable upbringing might see money as a tool for enjoyment and self-expression.

Although natural, these differences in financial behavior can lead to disagreements if we fail to appreciate and acknowledge each other's financial styles. It's essential to create a safe space where you and your partner can openly and honestly discuss money, including your financial habits, fears, and dreams, without judgment. These conversations allow you to see things from each other's perspective and find common ground, fostering a deeper understanding and harmony in your financial partnership.

Aligning Financial Goals

Before getting married, it is crucial to align your financial goals with your partner. Although money can be a sensitive topic, aligning your financial goals is essential to building a secure and fulfilling future. Let's explore some vital ways you can work together to align your financial goals and build a strong financial foundation.

1. Setting Joint Financial Goals

The first step in aligning financial goals as a couple is establishing common objectives for savings, investments, and major purchases. Setting joint financial goals is important to building a secure financial future for you and your partner. It allows you to work together to achieve common objectives and helps you avoid conflicts and misunderstandings about money matters. To help you set joint financial goals, here are some tips you can follow:

- **Start with a conversation:** Before you establish joint financial goals, it's essential to understand each other's priorities and values. Sit down with your partner and have an open and honest conversation about your financial situation, including your income, expenses, debts, savings, financial goals, fears, and dreams. This will help you both get a clear understanding of your current financial standing.
- **Identify your goals:** Determine your short-term and long-term goals. Your short-term goals include saving for a vacation or paying off credit card debt, while your long-term goals include saving for retirement, buying a house, or starting a business.
- **Create a plan:** Once you have identified your goals, it's time to create a plan to achieve them. Start by breaking down your goals into smaller, achievable steps and

assign responsibilities to each partner. Set specific deadlines and regularly review your progress to ensure you're on track.

- **Make sure your goals are realistic and achievable:** It's essential to set goals that are both challenging and attainable. Be honest about your income, expenses, and lifestyle to ensure that your goals are realistic.

2. Budgeting Together

The second step in aligning financial goals as a couple is to develop a shared budget that reflects shared financial goals and priorities. Once both partners have a clear understanding of each other's financial situation and goals, they can work together to create a joint budget. This budget should include all sources of income, expenses, and savings. It is important to prioritize expenses and allocate funds accordingly. For example, if buying a house is a joint financial goal, saving for a down payment should be a top priority. Here are some tips to help you budget together:

- **Track Your Spending:** Before creating a budget, you need to know where your money goes. Start by tracking your spending for a month or two to get a clear picture of your income and expenses.
- **Identify areas where you can cut back:** Once you have a clear picture of your spending, identify areas where you can cut back. This might include eating out less often or canceling subscriptions you don't use.
- **Allocate funds to your joint financial goals:** Make sure your budget reflects your joint financial goals by allocating funds to each goal. This will help you stay on track and motivated.
- **Review your budget regularly:** Your budget should be a living document you review and adjust periodically. Make sure you're staying on track and adjust your budget as needed.

3. Financial Planning

The third step in aligning financial goals as a couple is to create a roadmap for achieving your financial milestones together. Here are some tips to help you create a financial plan:

- **Define your financial milestones:** Your financial milestones might include paying off debt, saving for a down payment on a home, or investing for retirement.
- **Determine the steps you need to take to achieve your milestones:** Once you've defined your milestones, determine the specific steps you need to take to achieve them. This might include increasing income, reducing expenses, or investing more aggressively.
- **Create a timeline:** Based on your current income, expenses, and lifestyle, create a timeline for achieving your milestones. Be realistic about the time it will take to achieve your goals.

- **Adjust your plan as needed:** Your financial plan should be flexible and adaptable. Review your plan regularly and adjust it as needed based on your income, expenses, or lifestyle changes.

Division of household chores and responsibilities

One of the most common sources of conflict in any household is the division of chores and responsibilities. You may have experienced a situation where one partner feels like they're doing more than their fair share of the work, while the other partner feels like they're being unfairly criticized. To avoid these kinds of conflicts, it's essential to have a clear and comprehensive plan for how household chores and responsibilities will be divided.

Three key steps need to be taken to create a fair and equitable division of household chores and responsibilities. The first step is to define household responsibilities. You need to identify all the tasks that need to be done to keep the household running smoothly. These tasks include cooking, cleaning, laundry, grocery shopping, and childcare. It's crucial to be specific when defining these responsibilities so everyone is on the same page.

Once you have identified the household responsibilities, it's essential to determine your and your partner's roles and contributions. This process involves assessing your strengths and preferences and assigning tasks that align with them. Remember, household responsibilities should not be predetermined by societal gender roles. Everyone should contribute based on their strengths and preferences. For instance, if one partner enjoys cooking while the other hates it, it makes sense for the partner who enjoys cooking to take on most of the cooking responsibilities.

The next step is collaborative decision-making. This involves discussing how to divide household responsibilities fairly and ensuring you and your partner are accountable for your contributions. Consider setting up a schedule or a chore chart so both of you know what you're responsible for and when. It's essential to be flexible and open to feedback during this process.

Managing shared expenses

Managing shared expenses is essential to building a strong financial foundation in any relationship. However, it can also be challenging for couples. Money has the power to cause tension and stress in relationships. However, with careful planning, budgeting, and communication, it is possible to create a system that works for both partners.

1. Household Expenses

When managing shared expenses, the first step is planning and budgeting. This involves identifying all shared expenses, such as rent or mortgage payments, utility bills, grocery expenses, and transportation costs. Once you understand all shared expenses, you can create a budget and allocate funds accordingly. It is crucial to ensure that everyone involved is aware of the budget and agrees with allocating funds. Additionally, remaining flexible and willing to adjust as circumstances change is essential. For instance, if one person experiences a job loss or a pay cut, it may be necessary to reevaluate the budget and adjust the allocation of funds accordingly. Similarly, if one person's needs or preferences change, it may be required to revisit the division of expenses and make adjustments accordingly.

2. Joint Accounts vs. Separate Accounts

When it comes to managing shared expenses, one of the primary decisions you need to make is whether to combine your finances or maintain separate accounts. Both options have their advantages and disadvantages, and the decision ultimately depends on your personal preferences and circumstances. Joint accounts can simplify the management of shared expenses and ensure that both partners contribute equally since all the money is in one place. However, it can also lead to conflicts if one partner feels like they are losing control of their finances. On the other hand, separate accounts provide more independence and autonomy but require more communication and coordination to ensure that shared expenses are paid on time. It's crucial to maintain open and honest communication about your financial goals and preferences and to find a solution that works best for your relationship.

3. Fairness and Equality

Ensuring a fair and equitable distribution of financial responsibilities is essential for managing shared expenses effectively. This means taking into account various factors, such as income, needs, and preferences, when dividing expenses. For example, if one person earns significantly more than the other, it may be unfair to split expenses equally. Fairness and equality don't necessarily mean a

50/50 split of expenses. Instead, it's about finding a system that works for both partners and considers each partner's financial situation and needs.

One way to ensure fairness is to consider a proportional split of expenses, where each person contributes a percentage of their income towards shared expenses. For example, if one person earns $60,000 per year and the other person earns $40,000 per year, the person who earns more might contribute 60% towards shared expenses, while the person who earns less contributes 40%. This can help ensure that expenses are divided fairly based on each person's financial situation.

Another way to ensure fairness is to consider each other's needs and preferences when allocating funds. For instance, if one person has a medical condition that requires expensive medication, it may be fair to allocate more funds towards healthcare expenses. Alternatively, if one person prefers to buy organic food while the other does not, it may be fair to split the grocery bill based on the cost of their individual preferences.

In addition, having open and honest conversations about your financial needs and priorities is crucial. This helps ensure that everyone's needs are met and that no one bears an unfair expense burden. Listening to each other and being willing to compromise and make adjustments as needed are essential in maintaining a fair and equitable distribution of financial responsibilities.

Handling Financial Conflicts

Financial conflicts are common in marriages and can be challenging to resolve. To tackle these issues effectively, it's essential to take a thoughtful and collaborative approach. The first step is establishing an open dialogue with your partner, creating a safe and comfortable space to express your thoughts and feelings without fear of judgment. Active listening is also crucial during this process, as it helps you understand your partner's perspective and underlying motivations. Once you've established open communication, the next step is to identify the core concerns or root causes contributing to the financial conflict. This step may involve discussing past experiences and financial values or clarifying misunderstandings. From there, you can work together to brainstorm solutions that address the identified core concerns, being open to creative ideas and willing to compromise.

After reaching a solution, it's essential to agree on a concrete plan of action moving forward. This could include setting specific financial goals, establishing budgeting strategies, defining roles and responsibilities, and scheduling regular check-ins to monitor progress and adjust as needed. By following this approach and approaching financial conflicts with patience, empathy, and a willingness to work together, couples can effectively resolve disagreements and strengthen their financial partnership in marriage.

CHAPTER TEN

RESILIENCE AND ADAPTABILITY

MARRIAGE IS AN extraordinary journey with its fair share of obstacles and challenges. While love and commitment are the foundation of any successful and long-lasting marriage, there's more to it than just that. A strong and healthy marriage requires resilience and adaptability. Resilience is the ability to cope and adapt to adversity, trauma, or significant stress, while adaptability is the ability to respond to life circumstances with flexibility and openness. Couples who fail to cultivate resilience and adaptability in their relationships may find it challenging to navigate through the difficulties that come their way. They may become overwhelmed, stressed, and unable to cope with the changes and challenges, leading to dissatisfaction, conflicts, and the breakdown of their marriage. On the other hand, couples who possess resilience and adaptability can face the storms together, emerge stronger, and continue to grow and develop their relationship. They are better equipped to handle the ups and downs of life, and they can find meaning and purpose in their marriage journey.

In this chapter, we'll delve into the importance of resilience and adaptability in marriage, the factors contributing to resilience, and the practical steps couples can take to cultivate resilience and adaptability in their relationship. Whether you've been married for years, are newlyweds, or are planning on getting married soon, this chapter will provide valuable insights and guidance to help you build a strong and healthy marriage that can withstand life's challenges.

Understanding Resilience

In any marriage, it's normal to face obstacles and challenges. However, what sets successful and long-lasting marriages apart from those that fail is the ability to bounce back from challenging situations and cope with stress positively and constructively. This ability is known as resilience.

Resilience refers to the ability to adapt and cope with adversity, trauma, or significant stress. It is an essential element of any successful relationship, as it helps couples navigate the ups and downs of life together. Resilient couples are able to communicate effectively, problem-solve, and support each other through tough times. Several personal strengths, coping mechanisms, and support systems contribute to resilience in marriage. Some of the key factors include:

- **Positive Outlook:** Resilient couples tend to have a positive outlook on life, even during difficult times. They find meaning in their experiences and maintain hope for the future.
- **Emotional Intelligence:** Emotional intelligence is the ability to recognize and manage one's own emotions and the emotions of others. Resilient couples have high emotional intelligence and can communicate effectively with each other.
- **Problem-Solving Skills:** Resilient couples are skilled problem-solvers. They can identify the root cause of a problem, brainstorm solutions, and implement a plan of action.
- **Social Support:** A strong network of family and friends can provide emotional and practical support during difficult times. Resilient couples have a support system they can rely on.

Building Resilience

Cultivating resilience as a couple is crucial to building a healthy and long-lasting relationship. It involves creating a solid foundation of trust, respect, and emotional connection, which helps both partners feel secure and valued. To achieve this, it is essential to foster a safe and nurturing environment where both partners can communicate openly and honestly and actively listen to each other's needs and concerns.

In addition to these fundamental building blocks, developing coping mechanisms and strategies to navigate stress and setbacks as a team is also important. This means identifying potential stressors and finding effective ways to deal with them together. It requires both partners to be willing to support each other during difficult times and make compromises and sacrifices for the sake of the relationship. Maintaining an optimistic outlook on life is another crucial element of building resilience as a couple.

This involves focusing on the positive aspects of your relationship and your lives together and learning to appreciate each other for who you are. Celebrating each other's successes and being there for each other during tough times can help strengthen your bond and build your resilience as a couple.

So, how can you develop resilience in marriage? Building resilience in marriage requires intentional effort and a commitment to working together as a team. Here are some practical steps you can take to build resilience in your marriage:

- **Communicate openly and honestly:** Effective communication is crucial for establishing trust, respect, and a solid emotional connection with your partner. You and your partner should communicate openly and honestly to establish and maintain a healthy and happy relationship. This means expressing your feelings and needs clearly and respectfully while actively listening to your partner's perspective.

- **Develop problem-solving skills:** Another crucial aspect of a healthy relationship is developing problem-solving skills. Working with your partner to identify potential stressors and develop effective strategies to deal with them is essential. This means collaborating to brainstorm solutions, being open to compromise, and seeking outside support if necessary.
- **Cultivate gratitude and positivity:** Cultivating gratitude and positivity can help you maintain a healthy relationship. Focus on the positive aspects of your relationship and your lives, and learn to appreciate each other for who you are. Celebrate each other's successes and support each other during difficult times.
- **Practice self-care:** Taking care of yourself physically, mentally, and emotionally is also essential for your well-being and your ability to support your partner. Self-care means learning to cope with stress and setbacks in a positive and constructive manner.

- **Prioritize quality time together:** Make time for each other and focus on spending quality time together without distractions. This could include going on date nights, taking walks together, or enjoying each other's company.

Cultivating Adaptability

Change is inevitable in any marriage or relationship. Whether it's a new job, relocation, or the arrival of a new family member, life events require us to adapt and adjust to new circumstances. The ability to respond to these changes with flexibility and openness is what we call adaptability.

Adaptability is a critical component of a healthy relationship. In fact, it often goes hand in hand with resilience, which is the ability to bounce back from adversity. When we cultivate adaptability as a couple, we become better equipped to navigate the ups and downs of life together.

What does adaptability look like in practice? Adaptability is the ability to embrace change and adjust to new circumstances. It means letting go of old patterns and habits when they no longer serve us and embracing new ways of thinking and behaving. In a relationship, adaptability implies that both partners are flexible and open to new experiences. It means that you recognize that your partner is not static and that they may change over time. It also means that you are willing to change and grow and are committed to continuing to learn and evolve as a couple. How can you cultivate adaptability in your marriage or relationship? Here are some adaptive behaviors that can help you improve your ability to embrace change and adapt to new circumstances:

- **Discuss Flexibility:** Talk with your partner about the importance of being flexible and open to new experiences. Discuss how you can both work together to adapt to changes and challenges as they arise.

- **Be Open to Learning:** Be willing to learn from your partner and open to new ideas and perspectives. Embrace the idea that you can always learn something new from your partner, no matter how long you've been together.
- **Willingness to Compromise:** Be willing to compromise and find solutions that work for both of you. This means being willing to give a little to get a little and recognizing that sometimes the best solution meets both of your needs.

Enhancing Adaptability

Enhancing adaptability is a vital aspect of any relationship, and various techniques can help you hone your adaptability skills. Firstly, effective communication is essential in enhancing adaptability. When you communicate openly and honestly with your partner, you can better understand their perspectives and adapt to changes. You can share your thoughts, feelings, and expectations with your partner, which will help you, adjust to any challenges in your relationship.

Secondly, empathy is a vital element in building adaptability skills. Empathy allows you to understand and empathize with your partner's feelings. When you practice empathy, you can put yourself in their shoes and understand their perspective. This helps you better adapt to their needs and desires, which is vital for maintaining a healthy and robust relationship. Lastly, understanding your partner is critical to developing adaptability. When you take the time to understand your partner's needs, desires, and fears, you can adapt better to changes and challenges that may arise in your relationship. This will help you build a stronger, more fulfilling relationship with your partner.

Managing Life's Challenges Together

Marriage can be a bumpy ride at times, and challenges are inevitable in any relationship. However, how we deal with those challenges can make all the difference. The ability to work together with our partners, face obstacles head-on, and find solutions as a team makes the journey even more beautiful.

Couples may encounter various challenges in their marriage, including financial stress, job loss, health issues, or conflicts with family members. It's essential to approach these challenges with an open and clear mind and open communication. When facing difficult situations, it's easy to feel overwhelmed or alone. However, it's crucial to remember that we have a partner who is there for us and can tackle these obstacles together.

Clear communication is key in any relationship, especially when dealing with challenges. Don't hesitate to express your feelings and concerns openly and honestly with your partner. This will allow you to work through the problem together and find a solution for both of you. Clear communication is critical to any relationship, especially when dealing with challenges. Expressing your feelings and concerns openly and honestly with your partner is essential. This approach can help you work through the problem together and find a solution for both of you. It's also crucial to support each other during tough times. You can provide emotional support and encouragement to your partner, which can make a significant difference in how we navigate through challenges.

Overall, always stay optimistic and focus on the good things in your life. Rather than dwelling on the challenges, be grateful for each other and the things you have. If you struggle to navigate a particular problem, don't hesitate to seek help. There's no shame in asking for assistance, whether from a therapist, a religious leader, or a trusted friend. Sometimes, an outside perspective provides valuable insights that help you see things in a new light and find solutions you hadn't considered before.

Building Emotional Resilience

Building emotional resilience is an essential part of maintaining overall well-being. Emotional resilience refers to the ability to bounce back from difficult situations, adapt to change, and manage stress effectively. It does not come naturally to everyone, but it is a skill that can be developed and strengthened through various practices. Let's explore three critical practices for building emotional resilience: emotional self-care, expressing emotions, and seeking professional support.

Emotional self-care

Emotional self-care is about caring for yourself mentally, emotionally, and physically. It involves practicing self-awareness, recognizing your emotions, and taking steps to manage them in healthy ways. Here are some practices for emotional self-care:

- **Mindfulness Meditation:** Mindfulness meditation is an excellent way to cultivate self-awareness and reduce stress. It involves focusing your attention on the present moment without judgment.
- **Physical Exercise:** Physical exercise is another essential practice for emotional self-care. Exercise releases endorphins; natural mood enhancers that help reduce stress and anxiety.
- **Journaling:** Journaling is another great way to manage stress and increase self-awareness. Writing down your thoughts and feelings can help you process them and gain insight into your emotions.

Expressing emotions

Expressing emotions is an important part of emotional resilience. It involves being open and honest about your feelings and needs with yourself and others. Here are some practices for expressing emotions:

- **Active Listening:** Active listening involves paying attention to what others say without judgment. It helps create a safe and supportive environment for open and honest communication.
- **Assertiveness:** Assertiveness is the ability to express one's feelings and needs clearly and respectfully. It helps one communicate effectively and build healthy relationships.
- **Empathy:** Empathy is the ability to understand and share others' feelings. It helps you connect with others deeper and build stronger relationships.

Seeking professional support

Sometimes, emotional resilience requires professional support. Seeking therapy or counseling can help you develop the skills and strategies to manage stress and build emotional resilience. Here are some signs that it might be time to seek professional support:

- Persistent feelings of sadness or anxiety
- Difficulty managing stress
- Struggles with relationships
- Trauma or unresolved emotional issues

Nurturing a Sense of Gratitude and Appreciation for Each Other

Nurturing a strong sense of gratitude and appreciation is a crucial part of building a healthy and happy relationship. It requires actively expressing and acknowledging your partner's value in the relationship and recognizing and appreciating their efforts, qualities, and contributions. This can be done through verbal expressions of gratitude, acts of kindness, or small gestures that show appreciation. Cultivating a sense of gratitude and appreciation helps to foster a positive and supportive atmosphere within the relationship, enhancing overall satisfaction and connection.

Remember, these aspects of embracing change and growth as individuals and as a couple, continuously investing in the relationship through learning and exploration, celebrating milestones and creating new traditions, and nurturing a sense of gratitude and appreciation are meant to serve as a starting point. Each relationship is unique, and it is important to adapt and personalize these concepts to fit your specific circumstances and dynamics.

Celebrating Resilience and Growth

Recognizing and celebrating a marriage's resilience and growth is a beautiful way to cherish and honor a relationship's journey. It's an occasion to commemorate anniversaries, birthdays, or other significant milestones the couple has achieved together. It gives two people a chance to reflect upon their shared experiences, appreciate each other's efforts, and express gratitude for their journey as a couple. Showing gratitude and appreciation to your partner is essential to maintaining a strong and healthy relationship. You can demonstrate your gratitude with simple acts of kindness, such as saying thank you, leaving a love note, or doing something special to make your partner feel valued.

Another way to celebrate a marriage's resilience and growth is to reflect on the challenges that the couple has faced and overcome together. This might include times when communication was challenging; one partner faced a health issue or a financial setback. In addition to reflecting on challenges, celebrating resilience and growth can also involve setting new goals and aspirations for the future. For example, making travel plans, trying new hobbies together, or considering expanding the family can all be exciting ways to look forward to the future.

Ultimately, celebrating a marriage's resilience and growth is all about cherishing the journey you and your partner have embarked on together. It's about acknowledging and being grateful for the love, support, and companionship you have shared along the way. Whether through a romantic dinner date, a heartfelt conversation, or a thoughtful gift, taking the time to celebrate your relationship can help deepen your connection and strengthen your commitment to each other.

CHAPTER ELEVEN

FAMILY AND SUPPORT SYSTEM IN MARRIAGE

MARRIAGE IS UNDOUBTEDLY ONE of the most significant relationships in a person's life. It is a special bond between two individuals who promise to stay together in good and bad times. However, marriage involves more than just the relationship between two people. It entails the involvement and interaction of other people, including family members and support systems. Family and support systems refer to people who share a close bond with the couple and provide them with emotional and practical support throughout their married life. These systems can include parents, siblings, extended family members, friends, and even professionals like therapists and counselors.

Having a strong family support system can significantly impact the dynamics and resolution of conflicts in a marriage. Unfortunately, not everyone is lucky enough to have such support. When extended family members don't provide the necessary backing and instead take sides, it can add strain and complexity to an already challenging situation. This lack of support can make navigating conflicts difficult, leading to feelings of isolation and unfairness.

Therefore, understanding the role of family and support systems in marriage is crucial for effectively addressing and managing relationship challenges. It helps couples maintain a healthy and happy married life despite the obstacles they may face.

Importance of family and support systems

One of the most critical factors in a successful marriage is having a strong support system; family can play a crucial role. In fact, the significance of family and support systems in marriage cannot be overstated. In this context, let's explore why it is so important to have these systems in place and how they can help strengthen the bond between partners.

1. Emotional Support

Marriage is a journey full of ups and downs, and it's natural for both partners to need emotional support at some point. In such situations, family and support systems can provide the necessary support. They can offer a listening ear, provide advice, and offer comfort during tough times. Their emotional support can help the couple navigate difficult times and emerge stronger in their relationship.

2. Practical Support

In addition to offering emotional support, families and support systems can also provide practical assistance to couples. This support may include assisting with household chores, caring for children, or even providing financial assistance during challenging times. This practical support can ease the burden on the couple and allow them to focus on their relationship.

3. Shared Values and Traditions

Family and support systems can also help the couple by sharing common values and traditions. This can help the couple create a strong foundation for their marriage and provide a sense of belonging and community. When both partners share the same values and traditions, it can help them feel more connected and aligned in their goals and aspirations for the future.

4. Conflict Resolution

Marriage is not always smooth sailing, and conflicts are bound to arise. Family and support systems can assist the couple in resolving disputes and finding solutions. They can offer an outside perspective and help the couple see things in a different light.

5. Building a Support Network

Building a strong support network beyond the marriage is crucial for maintaining both partners' emotional stability and personal growth opportunities. This network can include various people, such as friends, extended family, professional counselors or therapists, religious or spiritual leaders, and support groups. Having individual friends and interests outside the marriage is crucial for both partners to maintain a healthy balance of independence and togetherness. It allows them to bring different perspectives, emotional support, and experiences back to the relationship.

To build a support network in marriage, it's essential to first identify the type of support you require and then consider who in your life can provide that support. It's crucial to have a diverse network that includes both family and non-family members. You can create this relationship by attending social events, joining clubs or organizations, volunteering, and participating in community activities. These activities provide opportunities to meet new people and create meaningful connections. When you find someone you'd like to include in your network, communicate with your partner about them and be open to their suggestions.

Nurture your relationships with the people in your support network. Make time for them and show your appreciation for their support. Additionally, be willing to reciprocate and offer support when they need it. Remember that building a support network in marriage is not a sign of weakness but strength. It shows that you are committed to your partner and willing to work together to overcome any challenges that come your way.

Understanding Family Dynamics

Family dynamics refers to the complex ways in which family members interact with each other. Every family has unique characteristics influenced by various factors such as culture, religion, economic status, and family history. When two individuals decide to marry, they bring along their own set of family dynamics and patterns, including values, traditions, and expectations. This can lead to a mix of enriching experiences and challenges. These dynamics can be positive, negative, or a blend of both, and they can significantly impact family members' emotional, mental, and physical health.

Couples with positive family dynamics feel safe expressing their thoughts and feelings to each other, and conflicts are resolved through healthy communication and compromise. Positive family dynamics can contribute to a sense of belonging, self-esteem, and overall well-being for both partners in the marriage. On the other hand, negative family dynamics involve unhealthy communication, disrespect, and conflict. Couples with negative family dynamics may feel unheard, unvalued, and unsupported, leading to emotional and mental distress. Negative family dynamics can also contribute to toxic stress, poor health outcomes, and strained relationships.

Understanding family dynamics requires acknowledging negative patterns and promoting positive ones. It involves active listening, empathy, and effective communication. Couples can work together to establish healthy boundaries, express their needs and feelings, and resolve conflicts respectfully.

Balancing Family and Extended Family

Maintaining a proper balance between external and one's own family is crucial in every marriage. However, sometimes, this balance can be a bit tricky to navigate. I remember feeling neglected, alone, and unimportant in my marriage because my husband failed to strike the right balance between both families. It felt like I constantly competed for his attention and affection. Still, I always came second to his extended family and ex-girlfriend. His family's close-knit bond was impenetrable, and I couldn't seem to be a part of it despite my best efforts. They were always there for him, supporting his choices and cheering him on. But for me? I was always an outsider, always made to feel like I was just a temporary addition to his life.

This behavior didn't just affect me; it impacted our children, too. They could sense the divisions within our family, making them feel like they had to pick sides. It was an unfair situation for everyone involved, and it left me feeling like I was losing my family. Sadly, there seemed to be nothing I could do to stop it.

As a devout Christian, I firmly believe in the Biblical principle of Genesis 2:24. The verse emphasizes the importance of a man leaving his parents and uniting with his spouse to become one. Unfortunately, my husband's behavior contradicted this principle entirely. He never allowed anyone, including his wife and children, to come between him and his family. This made the situation even more challenging and left me feeling hurt, confused, and alone. The experience was painful and emotional, and I knew I had to make a change, but I didn't know where to start. All I knew was that I couldn't continue living like this.

Finding a balance between family independence and extended family involvement can be challenging but achievable. It requires a willingness to prioritize your immediate family while simultaneously showing love and respect to your extended family. Prioritizing your immediate family is essential as it strengthens your relationship with your spouse. When you prioritize your spouse and children, you demonstrate to them that they are the most important people in your life. This helps to build trust, respect, and a deeper emotional connection in your marriage. Conversely, prioritizing your extended family over your immediate family can create tension and conflict in your marriage. Your spouse may feel neglected or unimportant, leading to resentment and distance in your relationship.

Achieving the right balance between family independence and extended family involvement requires clear communication, setting boundaries, and mutual respect. It involves having open and honest conversations with extended family members about priorities and boundaries, setting clear expectations, and being flexible yet firm in maintaining those boundaries. It also entails prioritizing quality time with our immediate family, protecting these moments from external distractions, and seeking support when conflicts or challenges arise.

Expectations Regarding Extended Family

Extended family dynamics play a significant role in shaping marital relationships. Understanding how these dynamics affect marital dynamics is critical to fostering harmony and addressing conflicts that arise from differing family values and expectations. When discussing expectations regarding extended family in marriage, both partners must communicate openly and honestly about their desires, boundaries, and values. Here are some points to consider:

- **Communication:** Couples need to communicate openly and honestly about their expectations regarding how involved their extended families will be in their lives. They should discuss how often they plan to meet their extended family, how they will prioritize family events and gatherings, and how they will handle conflicts or disagreements with extended family members.
- **Boundaries:** Couples should establish boundaries with extended family members to maintain a healthy and

happy marriage. They should discuss and agree on boundaries regarding financial support, decision-making, parenting styles, and personal space.

- **Support:** While extended family can be a great source of emotional support and a sense of community, couples need to prioritize their relationship and ensure that their marriage remains a top priority. They should discuss how they can support each other in managing relationships with extended family members and handling any challenges.
- **Cultural differences:** Couples who come from different cultural backgrounds may have different expectations about the role of extended family in their marriage. It is essential for partners to have open discussions and understand each other's cultural values and traditions. They should strive to find a balance that respects both partners' backgrounds and enables them to navigate their differences.

- **Flexibility:** As families grow and circumstances change, couples should remain flexible and adjust their expectations for extended family involvement in their marriage.
- **Seeking support:** If couples are struggling to navigate expectations regarding extended family in their marriage, they may benefit from seeking support from a therapist or counselor. A professional can assist them in effectively communicating with each other, setting boundaries, and finding mutually acceptable solutions.

Financial Considerations within Extended Family

Managing finances can be a challenging task for anyone, but it can be even more difficult for couples who have extended family members involved in their financial affairs. One of the primary challenges that couples face is managing the financial expectations of their extended family members. To address this challenge, it is crucial to establish clear boundaries and expectations regarding money with family members. Couples must understand what financial support they can provide and what support they expect from others. This can help avoid misunderstandings and conflicts that can cause strain and stress within the family.

Another important consideration is the impact that the financial dynamics of an extended family can have on marital finances. For instance, if one spouse financially supports their extended family members, this can strain the couple's finances. In such situations, it's essential to have open and honest communication about the financial support being given and to set boundaries to ensure that the couple's financial goals are not compromised.

Challenges in Family and Support Systems

While having extended family members as a support system can be incredibly valuable for married couples, it can also bring about conflicts and tensions that can be difficult to navigate. My husband and I experienced this firsthand while going through some serious issues in our marriage. It was challenging to balance the opinions and advice of multiple family members, especially when their input didn't align with what was best for our relationship.

In my case, my husband's sisters held a lot of influence over him, especially when it came to decisions that involved me. Conversations always seemed one-sided and favored him, even when he was wrong. Their unwavering support of his actions, even when they negatively impacted our children and me, left me feeling alone and unsupported. It's important to remember that while family can be a great source of support, you and your spouse must make the best decisions for yourselves and your family.

Moreover, when my husband's infidelity came to light, his family chose to cover it up instead of addressing it. This lack of accountability only worsened the situation by inflating his ego and making him even more difficult to deal with. Even his grandmother dismissed his behavior with the misguided notion that "all men cheat," advising me to simply accept it and love him while doing my own thing. Her words left me speechless and disillusioned, losing respect for her. Statements like these only normalize and enable infidelity, which can have devastating consequences for everyone involved.

Overall, my husband's family only added to the resentment in our marriage instead of challenging his behavior. They enabled him, making the situation even more challenging for me and our family. Couples need to set boundaries with their extended family and prioritize their decision-making process while still considering their family's input. They should also seek support only from those who respect their choices and have their best interests at heart, even if they aren't family.

Strategies for fostering harmony between extended family and marital relationships

Fostering harmony between extended family and marital relationships requires effort from both partners. Here are some strategies that can help:

- **Communication:** Open and honest communication is key to addressing conflicts and finding solutions that work for both partners.
- **Compromise:** Both partners should be willing to compromise and find common ground regarding family dynamics.
- **Boundaries:** Setting boundaries around the relationship with extended family can help create a healthy balance between family and marital life.
- **Respect:** It's important to respect each other's feelings and boundaries, including those of our families.
- **Seek support:** If conflicts become too difficult to manage on your own, seeking support from a therapist or counselor can help you navigate these challenges.

It's important to remember that challenges are a normal part of family life. With the right strategies, families can overcome these challenges and grow stronger together.

CHAPTER TWELVE

REASONS WHY 50% OF MARRIAGES OR RELATIONSHIPS FAIL

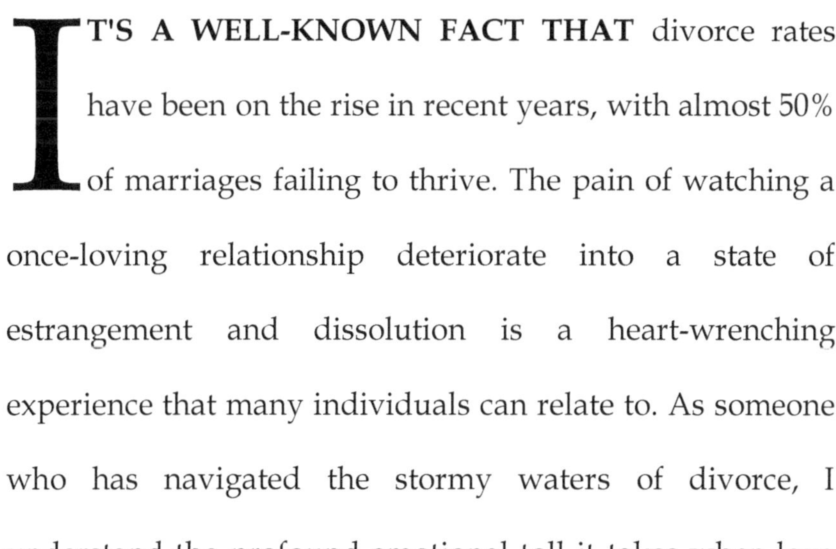

IT'S A WELL-KNOWN FACT THAT divorce rates have been on the rise in recent years, with almost 50% of marriages failing to thrive. The pain of watching a once-loving relationship deteriorate into a state of estrangement and dissolution is a heart-wrenching experience that many individuals can relate to. As someone who has navigated the stormy waters of divorce, I understand the profound emotional toll it takes when love turns into indifference and promises are shattered. Initially, love bloomed like a beautiful garden filled with passion, affection, and dreams of a shared future. Vows were exchanged, promising to love and cherish each other until death do us part. However, as time passed and challenges arose, cracks began to appear in the foundation of our relationship. Miscommunication, unresolved conflicts, and unmet expectations gradually eroded our once-strong bond. And then came the dreaded decision - to end the marriage, accompanied by unfulfilled hopes, shattered dreams, and the realization that despite our best efforts, the relationship couldn't withstand its trials.

But why? You may wonder. Why do people who were once in love divorce their partners? The reasons for this trend are numerous and complex. However, in this final chapter, we will delve deeply into these reasons and explore how you can avoid such failure in the future. You will learn how to build a strong, lasting, and fulfilling married life that will stand the test of time.

Lack of Communication

You must have noticed that communication is mentioned numerous times throughout this book. This is because communication forms the foundation of every marriage. A lack of communication is one of the most common reasons for failed marriages and divorces. When couples fail to communicate their needs, concerns, and emotions effectively, they may feel disconnected. This can lead to misunderstandings, disagreements, and even resentment. Over time, this can erode the trust, intimacy, and connection necessary for a healthy relationship.

Without regular communication, couples may also become less supportive of each other's needs and goals, which can further strain the relationship. The inability to communicate needs, desires, and grievances leaves partners feeling isolated and unvalued, paving the way for conflict and, ultimately, separation. That's why it's so important for couples to make an effort to communicate openly with each other regularly. This involves actively listening to each other, being honest about thoughts and feelings, and being willing to compromise and work together to find solutions. When communication is strong, relationships can thrive, and individuals can feel closer and more connected.

Infidelity and Trust Issues

Infidelity is a severe breach of trust in a marriage and violates the fundamental values of commitment, intimacy, and honesty. When one partner cheats on the other, it can have devastating consequences, causing immense pain, hurt, and mistrust between the partners. The betrayed partner may feel like they have been deceived, lied to, and taken for granted, forcing them to question their entire relationship. The emotional wounds caused by infidelity can be challenging to heal, creating a distance that strains the bond between partners.

Infidelity can lead to significant consequences, such as broken trust, emotional trauma, and even divorce. Trust is the foundation of any relationship. However, infidelity can shatter this foundation and make it difficult to rebuild. When trust is broken in a relationship, it can lead to many negative emotions, such as insecurity, jealousy, anger, and a lack of communication. Even simple interactions can become laced with doubt, making healthy intimacy nearly impossible. The betrayed partner may also feel like they have lost a part of themselves, and their sense of self-worth may be diminished.

The pain and betrayal that arise from infidelity can take a toll on a relationship, causing deep-seated resentment and frequent arguments. This can create a vicious cycle where partners lash out at each other, withdraw emotionally, or become distant and unresponsive. As a result, focusing on the relationship's positive aspects becomes increasingly challenging, making it all the more difficult to rebuild and repair what has been broken.

Infidelity may sometimes be a sign of more profound problems in a marriage, such as a lack of communication, unfulfilled emotional needs, or emotional neglect. When trust is broken, these underlying issues become more prominent, making it even more challenging to deal with them constructively. However, to address infidelity and trust issues, exploring the root causes that contribute to it is essential. This can involve seeking couples therapy, individual therapy, or both. It may also require taking a hard look at the relationship and adjusting to enhance communication, intimacy, and trust.

Financial Strain and Disagreements

Financial stress can cause a lot of tension and disagreements, which can negatively impact a marriage. Disagreements over money management, spending habits, and investments can also lead to arguments and resentment, which, if not resolved, can be a significant source of marital conflict, and in some cases, it can even lead to divorce.

When couples struggle with financial management, it can strain their relationship in various ways. The constant worry and pressure associated with financial stress can weigh heavily on both partners, leading to irritability, withdrawal, and reduced patience with each other. This heightened stress tends to spill over into different aspects of life, fueling disagreements, arguments, and underlying resentment.

Moreover, financial strain and disagreements can create power imbalances within the relationship. The partner with higher earnings may assume a dominant role, leading to power struggles and feelings of inequality. Conversely, the lower-income partner may feel dependent and insecure, complicating the dynamics. To navigate these challenges, couples should engage in open and transparent conversations about their financial situation and aspirations while respecting each other's financial attitudes. It's essential to establish a shared understanding of each other's spending habits, short-term and long-term financial goals, and the responsibilities of managing household budgets. Maintaining financial stability requires teamwork, trust, and mutual respect.

Lack of Compatibility

Compatibility is an incredibly important aspect of any successful marriage. When partners lack compatibility, it can lead to numerous challenges, including misunderstandings, arguments, and conflicts. Incompatible partners may struggle with effective communication, understanding each other's needs, and reaching compromises when necessary. These difficulties can result in frustration, resentment, and disappointment, ultimately harming a healthy and fulfilling relationship.

Some common signs of a lack of compatibility in a marriage include constant arguments, mismatched values, different life goals, and unmet expectations. External stressors such as financial difficulties, health problems, or job loss can exacerbate these issues. Individuals should examine their feelings, thoughts, and behaviors when interacting with their partner to identify compatibility issues. Observing their partner's behavior and communication style can also help determine compatibility. It's important to note that compatibility isn't about being the same but rather about having a shared understanding and respect for each other's differences.

Taking early action is critical to prevent a lack of compatibility from leading to divorce. Couples can seek counseling, improve communication skills, and work together to find common ground. Ultimately, it's up to each individual to determine what's most important in a relationship and seek partners who share those values and goals.

Unrealistic Expectations

Unrealistic expectations can be detrimental to any relationship, especially in the context of love and marriage. Often, people enter into relationships with preconceived notions about what their partner should be like and how their relationship should look. However, when these expectations are not met, it can lead to disappointment and dissatisfaction, ultimately causing the relationship to fail.

One of the primary reasons why unrealistic expectations lead to failed marriages is because they create a mismatch between reality and what one believes should be reality. This can manifest in several ways, such as expecting your partner to be perfect, thinking that they will fulfill all your needs, or anticipating that the relationship will be effortless. When these expectations are not met, it can lead to frustration, resentment, disappointment, and a breakdown in communication, trust, and intimacy.

Managing expectations in marriage and relationships is crucial for maintaining a healthy and happy relationship. This involves knowing your expectations and communicating them clearly to your partner. It also requires compromise and adjusting your expectations as the relationship evolves.

Cultivating realistic expectations and healthy relationship dynamics is key to a successful marriage or relationship. This involves being realistic about what your partner can and cannot provide, being willing to work together to solve problems, and being open to growth and change. In a healthy relationship, both partners feel valued, respected, and supported, and they work together to create a fulfilling and meaningful partnership.

Lack of Commitment

Lack of commitment can present itself in many ways in marriage. It may be a partner who fails to prioritize the relationship, struggles to communicate effectively, is unfaithful, or emotionally withdraws. Regardless of its form, it creates an imbalance that can be difficult to correct. When one partner feels neglected or unappreciated, it can lead to resentment, bitterness, and a breakdown in the marriage.

It's important to note that lack of commitment is not always a conscious decision. A partner may be going through a challenging time or experiencing personal issues that affect their ability to be fully present in the relationship. In those situations, both partners need to communicate honestly with each other to find a way forward. However, when one partner consistently fails to show up for the relationship, it's essential to address the problem before it becomes a complete breakdown. This may involve seeking the help of a therapist or counselor to work through the underlying issues that are causing the lack of commitment. Ultimately, lack of commitment in a marriage can lead to divorce. When one partner feels unsupported or neglected, it can be challenging to maintain a healthy and happy relationship. Both partners must be willing to work together to strengthen their commitment to each other and the relationship. This includes communicating openly, prioritizing the relationship, and seeking professional help when needed.

Emotional Intimacy

Emotional intimacy is a crucial element for a happy and healthy marriage. When emotional intimacy is lacking, couples may feel lonely, disconnected, and isolated, which can lead to a breakdown in the relationship and ultimately result in a failed marriage. The absence of emotional intimacy can also reduce physical intimacy, exacerbating the problem. Therefore, couples need to identify the factors contributing to emotional distance and detachment and work together to build a strong emotional connection, which is key to a fulfilling and successful marriage.

One of the primary factors that can lead to emotional distance is miscommunication. For instance, imagine a scenario where your partner is venting about their work, but you interrupt them with solutions. They might only want someone to listen to them without offering a fix. Active listening is a crucial skill that can help you understand your partner's perspective. You can achieve this by summarizing your partner's words and asking clarifying questions. Another factor that can contribute to emotional detachment is a lack of shared experiences. When couples do not spend time together or participate in activities they both enjoy, it can lead to feelings of isolation and disconnection. Additionally, unresolved conflicts and disagreements can contribute to emotional distance in a relationship. To maintain a solid emotional bond, it is crucial to address any issues or concerns calmly and respectfully.

To build emotional intimacy and connection with your partner, it is vital to prioritize your relationship and make time for each other. You can schedule regular date nights or plan activities that you both enjoy. It's also important to communicate openly and honestly with your partner and be willing to listen to their thoughts and feelings. Doing so can strengthen your emotional bond and build a long-lasting relationship.

Ignoring Red Flags and Unresolved Issues

Ignoring red flags and unresolved issues in relationships can have serious consequences. When problems are left unaddressed, they worsen and become more challenging to resolve. This can result in chronic stress, anxiety, and depression for both partners, eventually leading to a communication breakdown and the end of the relationship.

Recognizing the warning signs of a problematic relationship early on is essential. These signs may include a lack of trust, frequent arguments, disrespectful behavior, and a lack of communication. If you notice these signs, addressing them as soon as possible by having an open and honest conversation with your partner is vital. Seeking professional help, such as counseling or therapy, may also be necessary.

In some cases, it may be necessary to accept that the relationship is not salvageable. Although this decision can be challenging, it is important to remember that sometimes it is better to end a relationship than to continue struggling with unresolved issues and red flags. Ultimately, it is crucial to prioritize your emotional and physical well-being in any relationship.

Cultural and Societal Influences

The impact of cultural and societal influences on marriages can be significant, often leading to divorce. External pressures can become overwhelming, making it challenging for couples to prioritize their relationships and focus on each other's needs. Family dynamics, cultural differences, and societal expectations can create conflicts, misunderstandings, and resentment between partners. The stress of conforming to societal standards and pleasing others can also create tension and strain the relationship, leading to neglect and discontent.

In some cases, external pressures can even lead to one or both partners feeling like they have to choose between their relationship and their family, culture, or community. This can create a feeling of isolation and disconnection between partners, leading to further problems in the relationship. Over time, these issues can become too much to handle, and couples may choose to separate or divorce.

It's essential to recognize the influence of external factors on marriages and take steps to address them. Couples can work together to identify and navigate external pressures, communicate openly and honestly about their needs and feelings, and seek support from a therapist or counselor if necessary. By doing so, they can strengthen their relationship and overcome the challenges that cultural and societal influences can bring.

Overall, the reasons behind the high rate of relationship breakdowns are complex and varied. However, taking active steps to address these issues can help reverse this trend and promote enduring, fulfilling relationships. To achieve this, it is important to cultivate strong communication skills, manage financial pressures constructively, fully commit to relationship maintenance, align expectations, and navigate external pressures with unity. Understanding and tackling these challenges is crucial for strengthening your bond, enhancing resilience, and increasing the likelihood of long-term partnership success.

CONCLUSION

As we come to the end of "Before the Vow," it is important to reflect on what we have learned about relationships, finances, and the journey toward marriage. Marriage is not just a one-time event but a lifelong commitment to understanding, supporting, and growing with your partner. It entails facing challenges together, communicating openly and honestly, and building a future based on trust and mutual respect.

Whether you are planning to get married, newly married, or have been married for years, this book has provided essential insights to help you navigate married life confidently and clearly. From personal stories to practical advice and real-world examples, we have covered various topics to help couples merge their lives, finances, and responsibilities. We emphasized the importance of setting goals together, managing conflicts constructively, and fostering a strong foundation of love and understanding. As you prepare for your own journey into marriage, remember that it is okay to seek guidance, communicate your needs and desires, and continuously work on strengthening your bond. Marriage is a lifelong commitment that requires patience, understanding, and dedication. The vows you will exchange are more than words; they are promises to stand by each other, support each other's dreams, and face life's challenges as a team. So, walk down the aisle with your favorite partner, holding onto the knowledge that you are prepared to make your marriage successful and thriving. Building a healthy and fulfilling marriage takes effort, but with the right mindset and tools, you can overcome any obstacle and enjoy a lifetime of love and happiness.

I would love for you and your partner to take a moment to complete our marriage workbook. "Journey to a Successful Union" you will love it. It will help you to further put things into perspective. As you now know before entering into a serious relationship or considering marriage, it's essential to assess your readiness and suitability for a committed partnership. My workbook will guide you through evaluating various aspects of your readiness, including emotional preparedness, commitment level, communication skills, and conflict resolution abilities. By completing the exercises and reflections in my workbook, you'll gain valuable insights into your readiness to embark on this important life journey.

Thank you for reading my book and I sincerely hope that it fulfills you profoundly and abundantly.

www.ingramcontent.com/pod-product-compliance
Lightning Source LLC
LaVergne TN
LVHW020709110826
845149LV00012B/2184

* 9 7 9 8 9 9 0 6 2 5 4 0 2 *